PESTO

The Art
of Cooking
with Herb Pastes

Printed in USA

© Copyright 2013 KitchenAdvance

ISBN 978-1-938653-09-4

Table of Contents

Chapter 1

Making Pesto   **8**
    Classic Basil Pesto   17
    Basil Mint Pesto   18
    Purple Basil Pesto   19
    Basil & Watercress Pesto   20
    Basil & Sorrel Pesto   21
    Basil & Oregano Pesto   22
    Ricotta Basil Pesto   23
    Lemon Basil Pesto   24
    Pistachio Basil Classico   25
    Fennel Pesto   26
    Arugula Pesto   27
    Emerald Arugula Pesto   28
    Spinach Pesto   29
    Parsley Pesto   30
    Three Herb Pesto   31
    Oregano Pesto   32
    Cilantro Pesto   33
    Basil Lime Pesto   34
    Rosemary Pesto   35
    Garlic Chive Pesto   36
    Herb Bouquet Pesto   37
    Summer Savory Pesto   38
    Garlic Thyme Pesto   39
    Lemon Thyme Pesto   40
    Caraway Thyme Pesto   41

Table of Contents

Ricotta Caraway Thyme Pesto 42
French Tarragon Pesto 43
Tarragon Cream Pesto 44
Herbed Anchovy Pesto 45
Winter Pestos 46

Chapter 2

Pesto with Pasta 47
Linguine with Broccoli Pesto and Bacon 53
Cannelloni with Pesto Cream 54
Baked Shells with Ricotta & Pesto 56
Elbows and Tomatoes with 3 Herb Pesto 57
Grilled Chicken in Mint Pesto Cream 58
Pesto Lasagna 60
Linguine al Pesto 62
Pesto Marinara Sauce with Lobster 63
Angel Hair with Purple Pesto 64
Garlic Pesto Snow Peas with Pasta 65
Lemon Pesto Shellfish Sauce 66
Fennel and Sun-Dried Tomato Sauce 67
Red Ravioli al Pesto 68
Summer Savory Carrot Sauce 70
Tarragon Cream Salmon with Pasta 71
Tuna and Parsley Pesto Sauce 72
Tomato Anchovy Pesto Pasta Sauce 73
Fusilli, Sausage, Caraway & Pesto Cream 74

Table of Contents

Chapter 3

On the Side   **75**
Minted Pesto Butter   76
Spaghetti Squash with Basil Lime Pesto   77
Pesto Vegetables   78
Chilled Cilantro Lobster   79
Shrimp with Tarragon Cream Fraîche   80
Purple Pesto Ceviche   81
Zucchini Pesto Soup   82
Ricotta Basil Pesto Cucumber Soup   83
Minestrone alia Genovese   84
Vegetable Sorrel Soup   85
Herb Bouquet Soup with Mussels   86
Minestrone Verde   88
Pesto Chicken and Pasta Salad   90
Tortellini, Shrimp & Pesto Salad   91
Fennel Fruit Salad   92
Cilantro Pesto Pasta Salad   93
Continental Potato Salad   94
Red Ricotta Caraway Coleslaw   95
Warm Feta Cheese Salad   96
Tuna Green Bean Bouquet   98
Pasta Seafood Salad   99
Herbed Anchovy Pasta Salad   100
Pea Pods, Shrimp, and Barley Salad   101
Steamed Asparagus with Pesto Hollandaise   102
Purple Stuffed Tomatoes   103
Pesto Stuffed Mushrooms   104

Table of Contents

Mint Pesto Tabbouleh   106
Pesto Bread   108
Sun-dried Italian Plum Tomatoes   110

Chapter 3

Main Courses   113
Pesto Vegetable Calzone   114
Pesto Cheese Torta with Grilled Chops   116
Pizzette Basil   118
Three Herb Pesto Pizza   120
Savory Pesto Frittata   121
Fennel Vegetable Soufflé   122
Baked Sole with Watercress Pesto Sauce   124
Basil Rice Casserole   125
Grilled Lemon Chicken with Bowties   126
Oysters with Lemon Sorrel Sauce   128
Pesto Snapper Kabobs   129
Grilled Salmon with Lemon Basil Sauce   130
Emerald Scallops with Arugula Crumbs   131
Pesto Vegetable Bake   132

Chapter 4

More About Basil and Pesto Ingredients   133
About Basil   134
Harvesting Fresh Herbs   136
Other Pesto Herbs   137
Suppliers of Herbs and Specialty Foods   141

Chapter 1

Making
Pesto

"Classic" pesto is undoubtedly one of the world's great culinary pleasures. Made from fresh basil leaves, pale green virgin olive oil, a well-aged sharp sheep's cheese, garlic, and pine nuts, this sublime experience is usually enjoyed in summer months when fresh herbs are available.

In Genoa, Italy, in the Liguria region where pesto originated, fresh basil is available year-round. Genovese cooks used a mortar and pestle to grind the pesto ingredients into a smooth green paste hence the name *pesto*.

This delicious uncooked sauce, which is now fashionable in America, is among the oldest known Italian dishes, said to have come about from the combined influence of the Arabs, Persians, and Byzantines. The Genoese claim to make the best pesto, based on the highly aromatic properties of the basil that grows in their climate.

Classic pesto is made with unrefined olive oil, though modern tastes often prefer it made with lighter olive oil and sometimes butter. Like all Italian sauces, pesto should be added to pasta in conservative amounts.

Traditionalists claim that the only way to experience true pesto is to make it fresh with a mortar and pestle. The hand method results in pleasing texture and it is quite simple to do with a good marble, ceramic, or hardwood mortar and pestle. Nowadays, pesto is easier to contemplate made with a blender or food processor. A hand pounded pesto is, however, something which all those who love Italian food should try.

"Classic" pesto must be made with fresh basil leaves. In America there are many varieties, from cinnamon basil to licorice basil, and from lettuce leaf basil to sweet basil. What is usually sold in summer markets is sweet basil, which has large, crinkly leaves, and a more minty fragrance and flavor than the basil grown in Italy.

There are many variations on "classic" pesto. It can be made with or without pine nuts or walnuts, toasted or untoasted, with or without butter, or with the addition of a small quantity of parsley to quiet its natural sweetness. Some Italians add both Parmesan and Sardo Pecorino (made from sheep's milk), while others, the Romans in particular, are horrified at the mere suggestion of introducing Pecorino to pesto. Other recipes call for all Sardo Pecorino. According to some well-known Italian sources, pesto made with Parmesan alone is a concession to decadent, modern tastes. A blend is usually suggested, so cooks can experiment with their own variations and discover their favorite flavor.

You might wonder what the fascination with pestos is. Pesto is Italy's answer to Mexico's salsa picante - a spunky condiment that enhances innumerable dishes. It is added to soups and tossed with pasta. It also makes a fabulous stuffing for mushrooms or chicken breasts and tastes wonderful over fish. Grilled shrimp and steamed artichoke leaves dunked into melted butter mixed with pesto and a squeeze of fresh lemon juice are delicious. Melt pesto over corn on the cob, steamed new potatoes, or sautéed vegetables, and it certainly peps up vinaigrettes and sour cream-based salad dressings.

Not only can you enjoy pesto all year, you can also savor an enormous variety of pestos by mixing a selection of fresh herbs, greens, oils and nuts. We have included variations of "classic" pestos and recipes that use the pesto as a seasoning. Part of the fun of making pesto is experimenting with different varieties of basil and other fresh herbs. We have also included some unusual pestos that use more exotic or untypical herbs like cilantro, rosemary, mint, and lemon thyme.

The recipes featured in this book are both simple and elegant. You can tailor them to whatever herbs and vegetables are fresh and good in your area. High quality fresh ingredients are very important as a starting point, because your finished dish will only be as good as the ingredients you put into it.

When creating a dish, take a moment and contemplate the ingredients you are planning to use. Smell their aromas and taste them separately, then together. Notice how strong or mild each is, and imagine how they will taste together, and in what proportions they should be used. Is there something else that might combine well with these flavors? When all the senses are involved, preparing and cooking simple food becomes a fulfilling and wonderfully renewing experience.

There are really no rules in cooking, or in making pestos either. Like all recipes, these are really guides, so you must trust your own instincts. Herbs will vary in strength, taste, and flavors, depending on the seed, the soil, the weather, and when and how the herbs were picked. The garlic may be weak or strong; the oils and cheeses will vary. You, the cook, will gather all the ingredients together, taste, smell, and touch, devise a plan, and proceed.

Since we must agree that cooking is not an exact science, we must also recognize that amounts in recipes are suggestions to be used as you create a dish according to a sense of taste you've developed and learned to respect. The end results depend on using high quality fresh ingredients, getting involved and enjoying the food, and the continual tasting of your creation in progress.

The pestos are made from a variety of herbs, greens, oils, nuts, and cheeses. There is nothing complicated about the recipes or the process of making the herb pastes.

There are recipes for many different pestos, using basil, rosemary, thyme, tarragon, and other fresh and dried ingredients, but the basic method of preparation is always the same. Be sure to read the following sections carefully.

Equipment

A handmade pesto, pounded in a mortar with a pestle, has a silky, chunky texture that cannot be duplicated in a machine. However, using a food processor or blender really simplifies the time and effort in making pestos.

We recommend using a food processor for most of the fresh herb pestos, and the blender for making winter pestos, which are made with dried herbs. The tall, narrow container and blade of the blender helps to break down the firm dried leaves of thyme and rosemary, which do not seem to combine well with the food processor blade. A blender-made pesto will have a more puréed texture, but it is still a good sauce to make when fresh herbs are unavailable in the winter.

Herbs

No matter which fresh herb you are using, pick the leaves from the stem and measure the leaves first. Pack the leaves in a measuring cup.and measure before you wash. To wash the leaves, immerse them in a bowl of cold water and swish them around with your fingers to remove any dirt or grit. Rinse in a strainer or colander and gently pat dry with a paper towel, or spin dry in a salad spinner. Spread leaves on paper towels to dry further as you prepare the other ingredients.

When using herbs that don't provide a lot of green bulk, such as thyme, add a "green extender", such as parsley, for flavor, color, and texture. Italian flat-leaf parsley works best, but spinach, kale, watercress, sorrel, and other greens will work too. Added greens do have a tendency to dilute the flavor and intensity of the herb leaves. However, with strongly flavored herbs, such as rosemary and thyme, this is a good idea. Remember to wash and dry greens before being added to the pesto since water on the leaves will make the pesto runny.

Winter pestos are made with dried herbs so it is critical to use dried herbs that have a good strong aroma and are free of woody stems. The flavor of the winter pestos is very dependent on the quality of the dried herbs. Be sure to replenish your supply frequently since dried herbs have a shelf-life of only six months.

Garlic

Good fresh garlic cloves are a critical element in pesto. Elephant garlic can be used, but its flavor is considerably milder than regular garlic, so adjust the number of cloves. The fresher the garlic, the better the flavor.

Cheese

Cheese added to pesto must be freshly grated for full flavor. Buy the cheese in a chunk and grate it by hand or in the food processor with the grating disc, then the steel blade. You can store grated cheese for up to six weeks, refrigerated or frozen.

Since Italian Sardo Pecorino is mostly unavailable at present in the United States, a blend of freshly grated Parmesan and Romano Pecorino seems to provide the best combination of flavors.

Oil

Olive oil, with its flavor and viscosity, is the only choice for making pesto. A pale green, virgin olive oil (second-press oil), is recommended. The strong flavor of pesto is thought to be too overpowering for the deep green, extra-virgin olive oil, although it will certainly make a fine pesto.

Light-colored pure olive oil should only be used as an all-purpose cooking oil and is not recommended for pestos. The difference in flavor is tremendous because pure olive oil is made from successive pressings of the leftover olive pulp.

Heat and length of storage will affect the flavor so cap oil tightly and store it in a cool place.

Nuts

Pine nuts, or pignoli, are a traditional addition to the "classic" pesto. You may toast the nuts lightly (5 minutes for pine nuts, 10 minutes for walnuts in a preheated 300°F. oven) before adding them to the pesto.

Walnuts can be substituted in a basil pesto, but the milder pine nuts or unsalted pistachios should be used in delicate pestos, such as a Tarragon Pesto. Sunflower seeds and pumpkin seeds can also be used.

A pesto that contains noticeable pieces of nuts is very pleasing. A handmade pesto usually will have this textured quality. You can achieve somewhat similar results by using the pulsing action in the food processor and processing just until the nuts are well mixed but not reduced to a smooth paste.

How to Make Pesto

To make traditional handmade pesto, use a sturdy mortar and pestle, preferably made of marble or ceramic, that is large enough to hold all the ingredients. The better hardwood mortars are also good. Sprinkle some coarse sea salt or kosher salt and a few black peppercorns or freshly ground pepper from a mill into the mortar. Slice the garlic and add to the mortar. Crush the garlic, salt, and pepper, using a circular and steady motion to grind them. You will get a thick paste. The coarse salt will act as an abrasive to help puree the garlic and peppercorns. Add a few pine nuts and some basil leaves with a tablespoon of olive oil and continue crushing. Stir it all up occasionally. Add more leaves and nuts and a little oil. Continue crushing and stirring and adding the nuts, herbs, and a little oil. Too much oil will make it difficult to combine the ingredients. When you have added all the nuts and basil and have a fairly smooth paste, add the grated cheeses and oil, using the same circular motion until they are incorporated into the basil paste. Add the olive oil gradually, first in a trickle, mixing the paste with a wooden spoon. Beat the mixture continually as you drizzle in the rest of the oil. When it is incorporated, beat in the butter. You should have a thick purée. Taste for salt and season if needed. Let the pesto stand for a few minutes to allow the flavors to blend.

To make the pesto in a blender or food processor, combine the herbs, whole garlic and nuts in the bowl of the processor. Blend with the pulsing action, stopping the machine once or twice to scrape the sides of the container with a rubber spatula so that all the ingredients are equally ground. Add the grated cheeses and the butter and whirl for about 15 seconds. With the machine running, slowly add the olive oil. Season to taste with salt and freshly ground pepper. Scrape the sides again and turn on the processor for another few seconds. Continue to process until it reaches a good consistency as smooth or as chunky as you wish. Use the pulsing action to prevent over processing. Do not overdo the grinding or your pesto will have very little texture.

For a pesto that is almost as quick to make and with more texture, beat the grated cheeses and butter in by hand when you have finished processing the other ingredients.

Another version of pesto can be made by roughly chopping the herbs and nuts with a knife or mezzaluna(a two-handled knife with a blade shaped like a half-moon), or by using the pulsing action of the food processor. The garlic, freshly grated cheese, butter and oil should then be mixed in by hand. The rough texture with the herbs and nuts still apparent makes a very pleasing sauce for pasta.

No matter what method you make the pesto, allow it to stand for a few minutes before serving to allow the flavors to develop and blend. Just before serving or using pesto in a recipe, retaste and add salt and freshly ground pepper, if needed. Save some of the hot water from the drained pasta and stir about one tablespoon of it into the pesto. You can also toss the pasta with some butter (if you're not counting calories) before combining it with the sauce.

The pesto recipes in this book yield about a cup or so of pesto. This is more than enough for one pound of dried pasta or one full load of fresh pasta dough made into a specific shape with the Popeil Automatic Pasta Maker.

Keeping and Freezing Pesto

Pesto in a sealed glass jar will keep in the refrigerator for several months. The best way to prevent a dark layer from forming on the top is to push a layer of plastic wrap onto the very surface of the pesto. This is far more effective than the traditional method of pouring olive oil on the surface then sealing. When you are ready to use the pesto, spoon out as much as you need. There will be some discoloration of the pesto on the surface, but this will not affect the flavor. Simply stir the discolored pesto into the green pesto below. Recover with plastic wrap and refrigerate the remaining pesto.

You can freeze pesto in the same way. **But whether you are storing it in the refrigerator or freezer, it is important to leave out the cheeses, salt, and butter.** Beat them in just before using the pesto. There are those who also freeze pesto without the nuts and some who are satisfied with freezing completely finished pesto. You decide which method is best for you.

Freeze it in small quantities to make it easy to thaw in just the amounts you need. You can freeze pesto in 1/2-cup or 1-cup plastic containers, covered tightly. Or you can freeze pesto in serving size amounts on baking sheets covered with waxed paper. When the pesto is frozen, place it in small plastic bags to store in the freezer.

Classic Basil Pesto

This is our favorite version of "classic" pesto. Remember that you must balance the proportion of Parmesan to Romano to create the flavor you like.

2 cups fresh basil leaves
3 garlic cloves
1/3 cup pine nuts, very lightly toasted
1/2 cup freshly grated Parmesan cheese
scant 1/4 cup freshly grated Romano
OR Pecorino Sardo cheese
1/2 cup virgin olive oil
2 tablespoons sweet (unsalted)butter,
softened to room temperature
salt and freshly ground black pepper to taste

Combine basil, garlic, and nuts in a blender or food processor. Blend with pulsing action to mix. Add grated cheeses and butter and whirl for 15 seconds. With the machine running, slowly add the olive oil. Season to taste with salt and freshly ground black pepper. Continue to process until pesto reaches desired consistency. Allow pesto to stand for about 5 minutes before serving to allow flavors to develop.

Makes about 1 cup of pesto.

Basil Mint Pesto

The fresh flavor of this pesto can be served on the side with hearty meat stews or can be used to stuff mushrooms for a light appetizer.

**1 cup fresh basil leaves
1 cup fresh mint leaves
3 garlic cloves
1/3 cup pine nuts or walnuts, very lightly toasted
1/3 cup freshly grated Parmesan cheese
1/2 cup virgin olive oil
salt and freshly ground black pepper to taste**

Combine basil, mint, garlic, and nuts in a blender or food processor. Blend with pulsing action to mix. Add grated cheese and whirl for 15 seconds. With the machine running, slowly add the olive oil. Season to taste with salt and freshly ground black pepper. Continue to process until pesto reaches desired consistency. Allow pesto to stand for about 5 minutes before serving to allow flavors to develop.

Makes about 1 cup of pesto.

WINTER VARIATION: Substitute 1-1/2 cups fresh parsley for basil and 2 tablespoons dried for fresh mint. Slightly reduce oil. Blend according to instructions on page 48.

Purple Basil Pesto

Opal basil with sun-dried tomatoes makes an intense pesto that is great with pasta or can be melted over grilled fish or chicken. Garnish your dish with additional purple basil sprigs. See the recipe for sun-dried tomatoes on page 110.

2 cups fresh opal or "Purple Ruffles" basil leaves
2 teaspoons freshly minced rosemary
3 to 4 garlic cloves
1/3 cup pine nuts, very lightly toasted
generous 1/4 cup minced sun-dried tomatoes
1/2 cup freshly grated Parmesan cheese
3/4 cup virgin olive oil
1/2 teaspoon crushed dried red chili

Combine basil, rosemary, garlic, nuts and sun-dried tomatoes in a blender or food processor. Blend with pulsing action to mix. Add grated cheese and whirl for 15 seconds. With the machine running, slowly add the olive oil using a little oil from the sun-dried tomatoes. Add the dried red chili. Continue to process until pesto reaches desired consistency. Allow pesto to stand for about 5 minutes before serving to allow flavors to develop.

Makes about 1 cup of pesto.

Basil & Watercress Pesto

This mild, bright green pesto can be blended with a little cream and served with poached fish or steamed vegetables.

1 cup fresh basil leaves
1 cup fresh watercress leaves, stems removed
3 garlic cloves
1/3 cup pine nuts, very lightly toasted
1/3 cup freshly grated Parmesan cheese
1/2 cup virgin olive oil
salt and freshly ground black pepper to taste

Combine basil, watercress, garlic, and nuts in a blender or food processor. Blend with pulsing action to mix. Add grated cheese and whirl for 15 seconds. With the machine running, slowly add the olive oil. Season to taste with salt and freshly ground black pepper. Continue to process until pesto reaches desired consistency. Allow pesto to stand for about 5 minutes before serving to allow flavors to develop.

Makes about 1 cup of pesto.

Basil & Sorrel Pesto

The tart flavor of sorrel has been highly prized in European cookery for centuries, perking up soups, sauces, potato salads and baked fish with its lemony freshness. Try it over poached salmon or make the tasty soup on page 85.

**1 cup fresh basil leaves
2 cups fresh sorrel leaves, stems and vein removed
2 garlic cloves
1/3 cup pine nuts
1/4 cup freshly grated Parmesan cheese
1/3 cup virgin olive oil
salt and freshly ground black pepper to taste**

Combine basil, sorrel, garlic, and nuts in a blender or food processor. Blend with pulsing action to mix. Add grated cheese and whirl for 15 seconds. With the machine running, slowly add the olive oil. Season to taste with salt and freshly ground black pepper. Continue to process until pesto reaches desired consistency. Allow pesto to stand for about 5 minutes before serving to allow flavors to develop.

Makes about 1 cup of pesto.

Basil & Oregano Pesto

Oregano's spicy and peppery flavor is basic to many Italian tomato sauces and is beloved as the American pizza herb. This pesto makes a pleasing additive for sautéd summer vegetables and soups. Toss with salad greens, lemon juice and a little more olive oil, top with feta cheese, and you have a delicious salad.

2 cups fresh basil leaves
1/4 cup fresh oregano leaves
2 garlic cloves
1/3 cup walnuts
1/4 cup freshly grated Parmesan cheese
1/2 cup virgin olive oil
salt and freshly ground black pepper to taste

Combine basil, oregano, garlic, and nuts in a blender or food processor. Blend with pulsing action to mix. Add grated cheese and whirl for 15 seconds. With the machine running, slowly add the olive oil. Season to taste with salt and freshly ground black pepper. Continue to process until pesto reaches desired consistency. Allow pesto to stand for about 5 minutes before serving to allow flavors to develop.

Makes about 1 cup of pesto.

Ricotta Basil Pesto

The ricotta cheese gives this pesto a creamy texture. See the recipe for Baked Shells with Ricotta Pesto on page 56.

2 cups fresh basil leaves
2 garlic cloves
1/3 cup walnuts
1/2 cup freshly grated Parmesan cheese
1/4 cup ricotta cheese
1/2 cup virgin olive oil
salt and freshly ground black pepper to taste

Combine basil, garlic, and nuts in a blender or food processor. Blend with pulsing action to mix. Add cheeses and whirl for 15 seconds. With the machine running, slowly add the olive oil. Season to taste with salt and freshly ground black pepper. Continue to process until pesto reaches desired consistency. Allow pesto to stand for about 5 minutes before serving to allow flavors to develop.

Makes about 1-1/4 cups of pesto.

Lemon Basil Pesto

Lemon basil pesto especially enhances chicken or fish marinades and can be stuffed under the skin of chicken breasts before baking or grilling. It's also wonderful tossed with pasta, rice or steamed vegetables.

**2 cups fresh lemon basil leaves
3 garlic cloves
1/3 cup blanched almonds, lightly toasted
1/2 cup freshly grated Parmesan cheese
1/2 cup virgin olive oil
salt and freshly ground black pepper to taste**

Combine basil, oregano, garlic, and nuts in a blender or food processor. Blend with pulsing action to mix. Add grated cheese and whirl for 15 seconds. With the machine running, slowly add the olive oil. Season to taste with salt and freshly ground black pepper. Continue to process until pesto reaches desired consistency. Allow pesto to stand for about 5 minutes before serving to allow flavors to develop.

Makes about 1 cup of pesto.

Pistachio Basil Classico

This variation of the "classic" pesto can be served with any hot pasta and substituted for any recipe calling for a basil pesto. It uses only Parmesan cheese so it won't obscure the subtle flavor of the pistachios.

2 cups fresh basil leaves
3 garlic cloves
1/3 cup shelled pistachio nuts (unsalted),
very lightly toasted
3/4 cup freshly grated Parmesan cheese
1/2 cup virgin olive oil
2 tablespoons sweet (unsalted)butter,
softened to room temperature
salt and freshly ground black pepper to taste

Combine basil, garlic, and nuts in a blender or food processor. Blend with pulsing action to mix. Add the Parmesan cheese and butter and whirl for 15 seconds. With the machine running, slowly add the olive oil. Season to taste with salt and freshly ground black pepper. Continue to process until pesto reaches desired consistency. Allow pesto to stand for about 5 minutes before serving to allow flavors to develop.

Makes about 1-1/4 cups of pesto.

Fennel Pesto

Although sometimes mistaken for dill, the distinctive anise scent of fennel is unmistakable. It imparts a slight sweetness, crunchy texture, and mild licorice flavor to this pesto. The feathery stalks are a pretty garnish.

2 tablespoons fennel seeds
2 cups fennel root, bulb only
1 cup fresh Italian flat-leaf parsley
2 garlic cloves
1/3 cup walnuts
1/3 cup freshly grated Parmesan cheese
1/2 cup virgin olive oil
salt and freshly ground black pepper to taste

Discard the pithy stalks and cut the bottom off the fennel bulb. Roughly chop and steam for several minutes to slightly soften. Meanwhile, soak the fennel seeds in a cup of hot water. Combine drained fennel seeds, fennel bulb, parsley, garlic, and nuts in a blender or food processor. Blend with pulsing action to mix. Add the Parmesan cheese and whirl for 15 seconds. With the machine running, slowly add the olive oil. Season to taste with salt and freshly ground black pepper. Continue to process until pesto reaches desired consistency. Allow pesto to stand for about 5 minutes before serving to allow flavors to develop.

Makes about 1-1/4 cups of pesto.

Arugula Pesto

Arugula has a peppery taste with a nutty flavor reminiscent of sesame oil. This pesto makes a perfect topping for grilled fish.

2 cups arugula leaves, trimmed
generous 1/4 cup minced sun-dried tomatoes
1 garlic clove
1/2 teaspoon red chile pepper flakes
3 tablespoons sunflower seeds, lightly toasted
3 tablespoons freshly grated Parmesan cheese
1/4 cup virgin olive oil
salt and freshly ground black pepper to taste

Combine arugula, sun-dried tomatoes, garlic, red chili pepper and sunflower seeds in a blender or food processor. Blend with pulsing action to mix. Add the Parmesan cheese and whirl for 15 seconds. With the machine running, slowly add the olive oil. Season to taste with salt and freshly ground black pepper. Continue to process until pesto reaches desired consistency. Allow pesto to stand for about 5 minutes before serving to allow flavors to develop.

Makes about 1-1/4 cups of pesto.

Emerald Arugula Pesto

The creamy texture of this bright green and garlicky sauce partners perfectly with broiled fish or chicken. Or serve it on crackers or crudites. Decrease arugula and increase parsley for a milder flavor.

1 cup day old baguette crusts, torn in 1-inch pieces
5 tablespoons dill or white wine vinegar
3 tablespoons water
1-1/2 cups arugula leaves
1/2 cup Italian flat-leaf parsley
3 cloves garlic
2 teaspoons Dijon mustard
1/2 cup virgin olive oil
1 pinch brown sugar (optional)
freshly ground white pepper to taste

In a small bowl, soak the bread pieces in vinegar and water. Combine arugula, parsley, and garlic, in a blender or food processor. Blend with pulsing action to mix. Add the soaked bread and mustard and whirl for 15 seconds. With the machine running, slowly add the olive oil. Add brown sugar and season to taste with freshly ground white pepper. Continue to process until pesto reaches desired consistency. Allow pesto to stand for about 5 minutes before serving to allow flavors to develop.

Makes about 1-1/4 cups of pesto.

Spinach Pesto

Fresh spinach is not just good for you, it makes a truly delicious pesto. Use this pesto anywhere you would use a basil pesto.

2 cups fresh spinach leaves
1/2 cup fresh parsley leaves
1 garlic clove
1/4 cup pine nuts or walnuts
1 teaspoon dried basil
1/2 cup freshly grated Parmesan cheese
3/4 cup virgin olive oil
salt and freshly ground black pepper to taste

Combine spinach, parsley, garlic, nuts and basil in a blender or food processor. Blend with pulsing action to mix. Add cheeses and whirl for 15 seconds. With the machine running, slowly add the olive oil. Season to taste with salt and freshly ground black pepper. Continue to process until pesto reaches desired consistency. Allow pesto to stand for about 5 minutes before serving to allow flavors to develop.

Makes about 1-1/2 cups of pesto.

Parsley Pesto

This delightful variation on the "classic" pesto is perfect for when basil is out of season. Use flavorful Italian flat-leaf parsley.

**2 cups packed Italian flat-leaf parsley
3 garlic cloves
1/2 cup pine nuts or walnuts
1/3 cup virgin olive oil
1/4 cup grated Parmesan cheese
salt and freshly ground black pepper to taste**

Combine parsley, garlic, and nuts in a blender or food processor. Blend with pulsing action to mix. Add cheeses and whirl for 15 seconds. With the machine running, slowly add the olive oil. Season to taste with salt and freshly ground black pepper. Continue to process until pesto reaches desired consistency. Allow pesto to stand for about 5 minutes before serving to allow flavors to develop.

Makes about 1-1/4 cups of pesto.

Three Herb Pesto

This pesto is tasty over hot pasta, but also makes a terrific room temperature salad.

2/3 cup packed Italian flat-leaf parsley leaves
2/3 cup packed dill leaves
2/3 cup packed basil leaves
1/4 cup trimmed scallions, coarsely chopped
2 garlic cloves
1/2 cup walnuts
2 tablespoons fresh lemon juice
2/3 cup virgin olive oil
1/4 cup freshly grated Parmesan cheese
salt and freshly ground black pepper to taste

Combine parsley, dill, basil, scallions, garlic, and nuts in a blender or food processor. Blend with pulsing action to mix. Add cheese and whirl for 15 seconds. With the machine running, slowly add the olive oil. Season to taste with salt and freshly ground black pepper. Continue to process until pesto reaches desired consistency. Allow pesto to stand for about 5 minutes before serving to allow flavors to develop.

Makes about 1-1/4 cups of pesto.

WINTER VARIATION: Increase parsley to 1-1/2 cups. Substitute 2 tablespoons each dried dill and basil. Blend according to instructions on page 48.

Oregano Pesto

This unusual combination of oregano, lime and chile is excellent over a spicy flavored pasta or try serving on toasted baguette slices sprinkled with freshly grated Parmesan.

1-1/2 cups fresh oregano leaves
1 cup fresh Italian flat-leaf parsley leaves
3 to 4 cloves garlic
1/3 cup pine nuts, lightly toasted
1/2 teaspoon lime zest (avoid white pith)
1 teaspoon fresh lime juice
1 serrano chile, seeded and finely chopped
1/2 cup freshly grated Parmesan cheese
1/2 cup virgin olive oil
salt and freshly ground black pepper to taste

Combine oregano, parsley, garlic, and nuts in a blender or food processor. Blend with pulsing action to mix. Add the lime zest and juice and the chopped chilies. Add cheese and whirl for 15 seconds. With the machine running, slowly add the olive oil. Season to taste with salt and freshly ground black pepper. Continue to process until pesto reaches desired consistency. Allow pesto to stand for about 5 minutes before serving to allow flavors to develop.

Makes about 1-1/2 cups of pesto.

Cilantro Pesto

Cilantro, also known as coriander makes a pesto that is delicious over pasta. It mixes well with butter to drizzle over hot vegetables and is an excellent additive for dips, salad dressings and seafood.

1-1/2 cups fresh cilantro leaves
1/2 cup fresh Italian flat-leaf parsley leaves
2 garlic cloves
1/4 cup pine nuts, lightly toasted
1 teaspoon lime zest (avoid white pith)
1 teaspoon fresh lime juice
1/3 cup freshly grated Parmesan cheese
1/3 cup virgin olive oil
salt and freshly ground black pepper to taste

Combine cilantro, parsley, garlic, and nuts in a blender or food processor. Blend with pulsing action to mix. Add the lime zest and juice and blend again. Add cheese and whirl for 15 seconds. With the machine running, slowly add the olive oil. Season to taste with salt and freshly ground black pepper. Continue to process until pesto reaches desired consistency. Allow pesto to stand for about 5 minutes before serving to allow flavors to develop.

Makes about 1-1/4 cups of pesto.

Basil Lime Pesto

This basil and lime combination is a real treat over spaghetti squash. See recipe on page 77.

2 cups fresh basil leaves
3 garlic cloves
1/3 cup pine nuts, lightly toasted
1/2 teaspoon lime zest (avoid white pith)
2 teaspoon fresh lime juice
2 tablespoons sugar
1/2 cup freshly grated Parmesan cheese
1/2 cup virgin olive oil
salt and freshly ground black pepper to taste

Combine basil, garlic, and nuts in a blender or food processor. Blend with pulsing action to mix. Add the lime zest, lime juice and sugar. Add cheese and whirl for 15 seconds. With the machine running, slowly add the olive oil. Season to taste with salt and freshly ground black pepper. Continue to process until pesto reaches desired consistency. Allow pesto to stand for about 5 minutes before serving to allow flavors to develop.

Makes about 1-1/4 cups of pesto.

Rosemary Pesto

The aromatic, savory intensity of rosemary makes this pesto a delicious base for meat and vegetable marinades and robust salad dressings.

1/2 cup fresh rosemary leaves
2 cups fresh Italian flat-leaf parsley
3 garlic cloves
1/2 cup walnuts, lightly toasted
1/2 cup freshly grated Parmesan cheese
1/2 cup virgin olive oil
salt and freshly ground black pepper to taste

Combine rosemary, parsley, garlic, and nuts in a blender or food processor. Blend with pulsing action to mix. Add cheese and whirl for 15 seconds. With the machine running, slowly add the olive oil. Season to taste with salt and freshly ground black pepper. Continue to process until pesto reaches desired consistency. Allow pesto to stand for about 5 minutes before serving to allow flavors to develop.

Makes about 1-1/4 cups of pesto.

Garlic Chive Pesto

Garlic chives, also known as Oriental garlic or Chinese chives have flat, light green, reed-like leaves with a tasty mild garlic flavor. These chives are best in the spring when plants are young. Never substitute regular chives. Use additional stems for an attractive garnish.

3/4 cup fresh garlic chives, roughly chopped
1 cup fresh Italian flat-leaf parsley
1 small garlic clove
1/4 cup blanched almonds, lightly toasted
1/4 cup freshly grated Parmesan cheese
1/3 cup virgin olive oil
salt and freshly ground black pepper to taste

Combine chives, parsley, garlic, and nuts in a blender or food processor. Blend with pulsing action to mix. Add cheese and whirl for 15 seconds. With the machine running, slowly add the olive oil. Season to taste with salt and freshly ground black pepper. Continue to process until pesto reaches desired consistency. Allow pesto to stand for about 5 minutes before serving to allow flavors to develop.

Makes about 1-1/4 cups of pesto.

Herb Bouquet Pesto

This tasty conglomeration of Mediterranean herbs makes an aromatic pesto that can be added to breads or can spice up a basting sauce for lamb or chicken.

1-1/2 cups fresh Italian flat-leaf parsley leaves
1 tablespoon fresh summer savory leaves
1 tablespoon fresh thyme leaves
1 tablespoon fresh oregano leaves
2 tablespoons fresh rosemary leaves
2 garlic cloves
1/2 cup walnuts, lightly toasted
1/2 cup freshly grated Parmesan cheese
1/2 cup virgin olive oil
salt and freshly ground black pepper to taste

Combine parsley, savory, thyme, oregano, rosemary, garlic, and nuts in a blender or food processor. Blend with pulsing action to mix. Add cheese and whirl for 15 seconds. With the machine running, slowly add the olive oil. Season to taste with salt and freshly ground black pepper. Continue to process until pesto reaches desired consistency. Allow pesto to stand for about 5 minutes before serving to allow flavors to develop.

Makes about 1 cup of pesto.

WINTER VARIATION: Substitute 1 teaspoon dried herb each of savory, thyme, and oregano and 2 teaspoons dried rosemary and blend according to instructions on page 48.

Summer Savory Pesto

Summer savory's fresh taste is notable for perking up steamed vegetables such as green beans, squash, and artichokes. You can substitute the slightly stronger, peppery-flavored winter savory in this pesto recipe and use it in soups, stews, and casseroles.

3/4 cup fresh summer savory leaves
1-1/2 cups fresh Italian flat-leaf parsley leaves
2 garlic cloves
1/2 cup walnuts, lightly toasted
1/2 cup freshly grated Parmesan cheese
1/2 cup virgin olive oil
salt and freshly ground black pepper to taste

Combine savory, parsley, garlic, and nuts in a blender or food processor. Blend with pulsing action to mix. Add cheese and whirl for 15 seconds. With the machine running, slowly add the olive oil. Season to taste with salt and freshly ground black pepper. Continue to process until pesto reaches desired consistency. Allow pesto to stand for about 5 minutes before serving to allow flavors to develop.

Makes about 1-1/2 cups of pesto.

Garlic Thyme Pesto

Garlic lover's will want to use this pleasing sweet-flavored pesto as a base for pasta sauce or to spruce up an omelet.

1/2 cup garlic cloves
1/2 cup virgin olive oil
2 to 3 tablespoons fresh or dried thyme
1/3 cup walnuts, lightly toasted
1/4 cup freshly grated Parmesan cheese
1 cup fresh spinach leaves, coarsely chopped
salt and freshly ground black pepper to taste

Peel garlic cloves and simmer in olive oil on lowest heat for about 20 minutes. Do not brown. Set saucepan aside and let cloves cool in the oil.

Combine thyme and nuts in a blender or food processor. Blend with pulsing action to mix. Add garlic cloves and cheese, and whirl for 15 seconds. With the machine running, slowly add the olive oil reserved from simmering garlic. Season to taste with salt and freshly ground black pepper. Add spinach leaves and continue to process until pesto reaches desired consistency. Allow pesto to stand for about 5 minutes before serving to allow flavors to develop.

Makes about 3/4 cup of pesto.

Lemon Thyme Pesto

When slightly crushed, the leaves of lemon thyme are redolent of fresh lemons. Sauces for steamed vegetables, fish and poultry are especially enhanced by this pesto.

1/2 cup fresh lemon thyme leaves
1-1/2 cups fresh Italian flat-leaf parsley leaves
3 garlic cloves
1/2 cup walnuts, lightly toasted
1/2 cup freshly grated Parmesan cheese
1/2 cup virgin olive oil
salt and freshly ground black pepper to taste

Combine lemon thyme, parsley, garlic, and nuts in a blender or food processor. Blend with pulsing action to mix. Add cheese and whirl for 15 seconds. With the machine running, slowly add the olive oil. Season to taste with salt and freshly ground black pepper. Continue to process until pesto reaches desired consistency. Allow pesto to stand for about 5 minutes before serving to allow flavors to develop.

Makes about 1 cup of pesto.

WINTER VARIATION: Substitute 1-1/2 teaspoons of lemon zest (avoid white pith) and 2 tablespoons of dried thyme for fresh lemon thyme. Blend according to instructions on page 48.

Caraway Thyme Pesto

Caraway thyme has dark green, shiny leaves and a special sweet flavor that has been used for centuries as a basting ingredient for beef. Combine this pesto with butter for a vegetable sauce, paté, or basting sauce for grilled meats and seafood.

1/2 cup fresh caraway thyme leaves
1-1/2 cups fresh Italian flat-leaf parsley leaves
3 garlic cloves
1/2 cup walnuts, lightly toasted
1/3 cup freshly grated Parmesan cheese
1/2 cup virgin olive oil
salt and freshly ground black pepper to taste

Combine caraway thyme, parsley, garlic, and nuts in a blender or food processor. Blend with pulsing action to mix. Add cheese and whirl for 15 seconds. With the machine running, slowly add the olive oil. Season to taste with salt and freshly ground black pepper. Continue to process until pesto reaches desired consistency. Allow pesto to stand for about 5 minutes before serving to allow flavors to develop.

Makes about 1 cup of pesto.

Ricotta Caraway Thyme Pesto

Ricotta cheese gives this pesto a creamy texture that works well added to vegetable dips and creamy salad dressings.

2/3 cup fresh caraway thyme leaves
1 cup fresh Italian flat-leaf parsley leaves
2 garlic cloves
1/2 cup blanched almonds, lightly toasted
1/3 cup freshly grated Parmesan cheese
1/4 cup ricotta cheese
1/3 cup virgin olive oil
salt and freshly ground black pepper to taste

Combine caraway thyme, parsley, garlic, and nuts in a blender or food processor. Blend with pulsing action to mix. Add cheeses and whirl for 15 seconds. With the machine running, slowly add the olive oil. Season to taste with salt and freshly ground black pepper. Continue to process until pesto reaches desired consistency. Allow pesto to stand for about 5 minutes before serving to allow flavors to develop.

Makes about 1 cup of pesto.

French Tarragon Pesto

French tarragon, the most flavorful variety of the versatile herb, is the basis for this aromatic pesto. Use it to make the dressing for chicken pasta salad (see recipe page 90) or as a basis for seafood sauce.

1/2 cup fresh French tarragon leaves
1-1/2 cups fresh Italian flat-leaf parsley leaves
2 garlic cloves
1/2 cup pine nuts or walnuts, lightly toasted
1/2 cup freshly grated Parmesan cheese
1/2 cup virgin olive oil
salt and freshly ground black pepper to taste

Combine tarragon, parsley, garlic, and nuts in a blender or food processor. Blend with pulsing action to mix. Add cheese and whirl for 15 seconds. With the machine running, slowly add the olive oil. Season to taste with salt and freshly ground black pepper. Continue to process until pesto reaches desired consistency. Allow pesto to stand for about 5 minutes before serving to allow flavors to develop.

Makes about 1-1/4 cups of pesto.

Tarragon Cream Pesto

Use the flavorful French tarragon and add a little cream to make a light pesto that can be tossed with pasta and delicate seafood such as salmon.

1 cup fresh French tarragon leaves
1/2 cup fresh Italian flat-leaf parsley leaves
1 garlic cloves
1/2 cup blanched almonds, lightly toasted
1/4 cup freshly grated Parmesan cheese
3 tablespoons heavy cream
1/2 cup virgin olive oil
2 tablespoons fresh lemon juice
salt and freshly ground black pepper to taste

Combine tarragon, parsley, garlic, and nuts in a blender or food processor. Blend with pulsing action to mix. Add cheese and cream and whirl for 15 seconds. With the machine running, slowly add the olive oil. Add lemon juice and season to taste with salt and freshly ground black pepper. Continue to process until pesto reaches desired consistency. Allow pesto to stand for about 5 minutes before serving to allow flavors to develop.

Makes about 1 cup of pesto.

Herbed Anchovy Pesto

The strong, salty flavor of anchovies in this pesto blends well with summer vegetables. Add lemon juice and wine vinegar for a tasty dressing for a seafood salad (see recipe page 99). For a milder version that tosses well with spaghetti and sun-dried tomatoes, substitute chopped sardine fillets and add salt to taste.

**1-1/2 to 2 tablespoons chopped anchovy fillets
1 cup fresh Italian flat-leaf parsley leaves
2 garlic cloves
1 tablespoon dried oregano
1 tablespoon dried thyme
1/3 cup pine nuts, lightly toasted
1/4 cup freshly grated Parmesan cheese
1/3 cup virgin olive oil
freshly ground black pepper to taste**

Combine anchovies, parsley, garlic, oregano, thyme, and nuts in a blender or food processor. Blend with pulsing action to mix. Add cheese and whirl for 15 seconds. With the machine running, slowly add the olive oil. Season to taste with freshly ground black pepper. Continue to process until pesto reaches desired consistency. Allow pesto to stand for about 5 minutes before serving to allow flavors to develop.

Makes about 1 cup of pesto.

Winter Pestos

Fresh herbs are not as readily available in the winter, however many markets now carry fresh herbs from around the world where growing seasons are opposite to ours. Many cooks have learned to grow herbs indoors, so they have a constant supply during the cold winter months. But when fresh herbs are just not available, a winter variation will do nicely. A blender is recommended for grinding the firmer dried herbs even though the resulting pesto has a more puréed texture.

Some of the recipes in this book have a winter variation at the bottom of the page. Or you can experiment by substituting a reduced quantity of dried herbs for fresh and adding additional parsley (available year around) to make up for lost bulk. Follow these instructions to turn just about any pesto into its winter variation. The yield will be slightly less.

WINTER PESTO RECIPE INSTRUCTIONS

Combine herbs, garlic, and nuts in a blender. Blend with pulsing action to mix. Add cheese and blend for 15 seconds. With the machine running, slowly add the olive oil. Season to taste with salt and freshly ground black pepper. Continue to process until pesto reaches desired consistency. Allow pesto to stand for about 5 minutes before serving to allow flavors to develop.

Chapter 2

Pesto
with
Pasta

Pesto and pasta are a perfect combination, simple to prepare and so satisfying that they make the perfect choice for quick family dining. And yet, these same dishes can be served confidently to your most sophisticated guests at your most elegant party. With a small collection of pestos in the refrigerator and a good pasta at hand, you are prepared for just about any dining possibility.

MAKING PESTO SAUCES FOR PASTA

Pestos are surprisingly fast and easy to make. Although they are considered the height of sophisticated Continental cuisine, most recipes can be put together in a matter of a few minutes and are delicious with pasta. They can be kept refrigerated or frozen until you want to use them.

You'll need about 3 to 4 tablespoons of pesto for every 1/4 pound of cooked pasta. While the pasta cooks, thin the pesto with a few tablespoons of the pasta cooking water (refrigerated pestos should be brought to room temperature). Then toss the hot pasta with the thinned pesto and serve it in a heated serving bowl. Two or three tablespoons of soft butter instead of the hot pasta water can be added to the pesto to make an even richer sauce if you're not counting calories. Some prefer to add a few tablespoons of heavy cream to the pesto before tossing with the pasta.

If you do add cream to the pesto, you may wish to heat the pesto just a little. Don't overheat or you will lose some color and flavor. Heat the pesto in a double boiler, and never allow the pesto to come to a boil. Then toss the warmed pesto with the hot pasta and serve in a heated dish.

Fresh Parmesan cheese should always be served at the table with pasta and most salads, with the exception of some of the more delicate pestos, such as Tarragon Pesto. Also, a good peppermill on the table is an absolute necessity.

It's really easy to create new sauces using pesto as a base. Look for something fresh and delicious at the grocery store that can be added to the pesto. Or look for small bits and pieces of meat or fish in your refrigerator that will add depth and variety to your pesto. Or maybe some finely chopped sautéed red peppers, young peas, mushrooms, or broccoli could be added. Bits of ripe cherry tomato, a little ricotta cheese, steamed mussels, or smoked fish are all things that can make a wonderful sauce that develops into a fantastic dinner, all from your simple little pesto.

About Pasta

Pasta is an international dish found in many cultures. It comes in a multitude of shapes and sizes. It's a challenge to identify them all. The Italian cuisine actually is made up of a number of regional cuisines, and each has its own name for the various pasta forms. Manufacturers have added new twists to the names. In addition to the Italian pastas, there are Chinese egg noodles, buckwheat noodles, and spaetzle—all delicious with pesto.

Experienced pasta cooks know their pasta shapes, although not all always agree on all things. The general rule is: use ribbed pasta or pasta with indentations (any of the rigati family, fusilli, or rotelie) that will "hold" the sauce with less thick sauces, and use tubular pasta with smooth surfaces (penne, ziti, or mezzani) with thick sauces that can cling. The shapes of the other ingredients are also important. Vegetables should be cut to match the shape of the pasta. Cut vegetables in a fine julienne, for example, when the pasta is spaghetti or linguine; vegetables like broccoli and cauliflower should be cut in florets and matched with boxy shapes like shells or radiatore.

There are hundreds of pasta shapes and many more names. In Italy, for instance, the very same shapes are given different names in different regions. The following list describes just a few of these shapes, most of which work especially well with pestos.

PASTA SHAPES

ANGEL HAIR: Very fine, thin long pasta .

BOWTIES: The American version of Italian farfelle, or "butterflies"; often egg noodle dough.

CAVATELLI: A short curled noodle, available fresh, frozen, and dried; the dried are shell-shaped with a slightly ruffled outside.

FARFELLE: See Bowties.

FETTUCCINE: Narrow flat noodles, about 5/8 inch wide.

FUSILLI: A long fat solid spiral spaghetti, or a short fat screwlike pasta similar to rotelie.

GEMELLI: Means "twins," because it looks like two short fat pieces of spaghetti twisted together.

LINGUINE: Narrow flat noodles, about 1/8 inch wide

MEZZANI: A tubular pasta 1 to 2 inches long with a smooth exterior the same pasta with a ridged exterior is called mezzani rigati.

MOSTACCIOLI: Means "small mustaches," but looks like penne.

ORECCHIETTE: "Little ears," which are round fat little (about 1/2-inch) saucer-like disks.

PENNE: A tubular pasta, about 1-1/2 inches in length; the ends are cut diagonally to resemble a quill or a pen point. Smooth exterior or ridged (rigati).

RADIATORE: A short fat pasta shape rippled and

ringed like a radiator.

RAVIOLI: Square filled pasta, about 1 inch square.

RIGATONI: Very large grooved tubular pasta.

ROTELIE: A short (1-1/2 to 2-inch) fat screwlike shape; sometimes called fusilli.

SHELLS: Available from tiny to jumbo; called conchiglie and maruzze.

SPAGHETTI: Round long pasta, about 1/16 inch wide.

SPAETZLE: Small dumpling bits, about 1/2 inch long.

TAGLIARINI: Narrow flat noodles, about 1/16 inch wide.

TAGLIATELLE:: Narrow flat noodles, about 1/4 inch wide.

TORTELLINI: Small curled, filled pasta, about 1 inch long.

TUBETTI: Narrow short tubes, about 3/4 inch long.

ZITI: A large tubular macaroni, slightly curved, called "bridegrooms."

COOKING PASTA

Pasta should be cooked in lots of boiling water. Although you might do with less water than what is recommended, which usually means using a stock pot or large kettle, you'll at least need a large pot which holds 4 to 4-1/2 quarts for cooking one pound of pasta. Fill the pot to three-quarters of its capacity. Add salt and bring the water to a boil. Adding a little oil to the water helps to prevent it from frothing on the surface and boiling over rapidly. Cooking in too little water will cause the noodles to stick together regardless of how much oil you may add to the water. When the water has reached a rolling boil, add the pasta, a little at a time, then stir it slightly and let the water return to a boil. Be ready to reduce the heat, to prevent it from boiling over.

Cook fresh pasta anywhere from 15 seconds to

3 minutes. Dried pasta takes between 2 and 12 minutes depending on shape and thickness. Time your sauce so that it is ready when the pasta finishes cooking. The pasta will become soft and gluey if it waits too long.

DONENESS

When cooked, the pasta should be firm yet tender, or *al dente* (literally "to the tooth") but not soft or sticky. When you cook pasta too long, it absorbs too much cooking liquid. As a result, when sauce is added, the dish can become weepy or watery. Pasta that is still a little firm is more likely to absorb some of the liquid from the sauce, thus preventing a soggy finished dish.

A long wooden spoon is helpful to stir and separate the pasta strands because it does not tear the pasta or conduct heat. The only successful way to cook pasta is to taste the strands continually.

When the "just tender" stage is reached the pasta is done. It should have only a slight bit of uncooked core to be truly al dente. Drain the cooked pasta at once, pouring it into a large strainer. A large pasta pot with a colander insert allows you to lift the pasta out of the boiling water at just the proper moment. Place drained pasta in a heated serving bowl and toss with pesto sauce. Serve at once.

If you are going to hold the pasta before serving (not recommended, but sometimes unavoidable) or if you are cooking the pasta for a salad, you should rinse it. Use lukewarm water and toss the pasta with a little olive oil to keep the strands separated.

Linguine with Broccoli Pesto and Bacon

1 pound dry or 1 load of spinach linguine
8 slices of bacon
2 tablespoons olive oil
2 tablespoons butter
4 cups small broccoli florets
1/2 cup Pistachio Basil Classico (page 25)
1/3 cup pine nuts
1/3 cup freshly grated Parmesan cheese
salt and freshly ground pepper to taste

Cook pasta until al dente, drain well, and toss with 1 tablespoon of the olive oil and set aside. Meanwhile, finely chop bacon. Fry, stirring occasionally, until crisp. Remove from pan, drain on paper towel, and set aside.

Heat the olive oil and butter in a sauté pan, and sauté broccoli for about 2 minutes, stirring frequently. Continue stirring and sautéing until the broccoli is barely soft.

Add the pesto and drained linguine to the broccoli in the sauté pan. Stir over a low heat for 2 to 3 minutes. Add the reserved bacon, pine nuts, grated cheese, salt, and freshly ground pepper to taste. Serve immediately and pass with freshly grated Parmesan cheese. Serves 4 to 6.

Cannelloni with Pesto Cream

This dish can be prepared up to a day in advance. Cover and store in the refrigerator until ready to bake.

16 sheets dry or fresh spinach lasagna

SPINACH FILLING

**2 teaspoons olive oil
1 onion, chopped
2 cloves garlic, crushed
12 fresh spinach leaves, shredded
1/2 pound button mushrooms, finely chopped
1 cup tomato purée**

PESTO CREAM

**3/4 cup Oregano Pesto (page 32)
1 tablespoon sour cream
1 cup yogurt
freshly ground black pepper to taste**

To make filling, heat oil in a frying pan over a medium heat, add onion and garlic and cook, stirring, for 3 minutes or until onion is soft. Add spinach and mushrooms and cook for 4 minutes longer. Stir in tomato purée, bring to simmering and cook, stirring occasionally, for 10-15 minutes

or until liquid evaporates.

To make Pesto Cream, place pesto, sour cream, yogurt and black pepper to taste in a bowl and mix thoroughly to combine.

Cook lasagna sheets in until al dente. Drain well.

Place spoonfuls of filling along one long edge of each lasagna sheet and roll up. Place rolls joint side down in a greased, ovenproof ceramic baking dish. spoon Pesto Cream over the top. Bake for 25-30 minutes or until hot and bubbling. Serves 4 to 6.

Baked Shells with Ricotta & Pesto

Use "Classic" Pesto in this adaptation of baked ziti. It is a great way to use up leftover pesto.

> **1 pound dry pasta or 1 full load of fresh pasta**
> **1/2 cup Classic Basil Pesto (page 17)**
> **1 cup ricotta cheese**
> **3/4 pound mozzarella cheese, shredded**
> **salt and freshly ground black pepper to taste**
> **1/4 cup olive oil**
> **1/4 cup freshly grated Parmesan cheese**

Cook pasta until al dente and drain.

In a large bowl, stir together the pesto, ricotta, all but 1/2 cup of the mozzarella, and salt and black pepper to taste. Add the pasta and stir to blend. Pour into a 10-inch square or a 1-1/2 quart shallow baking dish. Sprinkle the top with the remaining mozzarella and Parmesan.

Bake in a 350°F oven for 30 minutes, or until cheese is melted and bubbly.

Elbows and Cherry Tomatoes with Three Herb Pesto

This elbow dish is especially pretty if very small red and yellow cherry tomatoes are in season. It is served hot, but also makes a terrific room temperature salad.

**1 pound dry or 1 load of fresh elbow macaroni
about 1 cup Three Herb Pesto (page 31)
1 pint small cherry tomatoes, stems removed
(use half red and half yellow, if available)
1/4 cup chopped walnuts
freshly grated Parmesan cheese**

Place pesto in a large serving bowl.

Meanwhile, cook the elbow macaroni until al dente, or firm to the bite. With a ladle, carefully remove 1/2 cup of the macaroni cooking liquid; add to pesto. Drain macaroni. Add immediately to pesto. Stir to coat. Stir in the remaining 1/4 cup walnuts and the cherry tomatoes. Serve while still hot or at room temperature for a salad. Pass with freshly grated Parmesan cheese.

Grilled Chicken in Mint Pesto Cream with Farfelle

Farfelle, or butterflies, are the perfect pasta to drench with this creamy sauce with a hint of mint.

MINTED PESTO BUTTER

1/2 cup Basil Mint Pesto (page 18)
1 green onion (including top), sliced
pinch of ground nutmeg
1/4 cup butter, softened to room temperature

Combine pesto, green onion, nutmeg and butter in a blender or food processor. Whirl until well combined, scraping sides of container several times. Set aside.

1/4 cup pine nuts
2 whole chicken breasts (about 1 pound each),
skinned, boned, and split
1 tablespoon olive oil
1 pound dry or 1 load of fresh butterfly pasta
1/4 cup dry white wine
1 cup whipping cream
2 tablespoons chopped roasted red pepper
fresh basil sprigs
1/2 cup freshly grated Parmesan cheese

Stir pine nuts in a small flying pan over medium low heat until lightly browned (about 3 minutes). Set aside.

Rinse chicken and pat dry. Brush on all sides with olive oil. Place a ridged cooktop grill pan over medium heat; heat until a drop of water dances on the surface. Place chicken on hot pan and cook, turning once, until well browned on outside and no longer pink in center; cut in thickest part to test (about 10 minutes total). Cut chicken into 1/2-inch-wide bite size strips.

While chicken is cooking, cook pasta until al dente. Drain well and set aside.

In a wide frying pan, combine Minted Pesto Butter and wine. Cook over medium heat, stirring occasionally, until bubbly (about 2 minutes). Stir in cream and bring to a full rolling boil, stirring often. Season sauce to taste with salt, then add roasted pepper, pasta, and chicken. Mix gently, using 2 spoons. Sprinkle mixture with toasted pine nuts and garnish with fresh basil sprigs. Serve with Parmesan cheese. Serves 4 to 6.

Pesto Lasagna

Folding pesto into ricotta and layering in between lasagna noodles is wonderful use for this rich Pesto.

TOMATO SAUCE

1 clove garlic, chopped
1 tablespoon olive oil
1 pound fresh tomatoes OR
1 (14-1/2 ounce) can plum tomatoes
1/2 teaspoon dried oregano
2 tablespoons of fresh parsley
salt and freshly ground black pepper to taste

Sauté garlic in olive oil. If using fresh tomatoes, remove skin by blanching in water for 30 seconds. Then cut off stem end and squeeze out seeds. If using canned tomatoes, drain the liquid. Chop tomatoes and add to pan with garlic along with remaining ingredients. Bring to a boil and simmer uncovered for about 10 minutes.

1 pound spinach or plain lasagna noodles
2 (15 ounce) containers ricotta cheese
2 slices bacon, chopped
1/2 pound ground sirloin
1/2 cup chicken livers, chopped
2 eggs
freshly ground black pepper to taste

1/2 cup Rosemary Pesto (page 35)
1/3 cup olive oil
1/2 cup freshly grated Parmesan cheese
2 cups Italian Fontina OR
mozzarella cheese, shredded

While tomato sauce is cooking, cook lasagna noodles and drain. Let noodles sit in a bowl of cool water until ready to use.

Meanwhile, sauté bacon, ground sirloin and chicken livers in a large pan. Drain and add to reserved tomato sauce, mixing well.

In a bowl, beat ricotta, eggs, and pepper until blended; fold in the pesto until blended. Heat oven to 350°F. Select a 9 x 13 inch shallow baking pan. Lift the noodles from the water individually and blot dry on paper toweling. Arrange 4 noodles in a slightly overlapping layer in the bottom of the dish.

Spread half of the ricotta mixture and half the tomato sauce mixture over the noodles. Sprinkle with 1/2 cup of the shredded Fontina cheese. Arrange a second layer of 4 slightly overlapping lasagna noodles on top of the ricotta mixture. Spread the remaining ricotta mixture on top, sprinkle with 1/2 cup of the Fontina. Arrange a third layer of 4 slightly overlapping lasagna on top. Spoon the remaining tomato sauce over the top and sprinkle with the remaining 1 cup shredded Fontina cheese.

Linguine al Pesto

In this recipe potatoes and green beans, classic Genoese additions, are cooked with the pasta providing a pleasing contrast to the richness of the pesto.

**1 russet potato, peeled and diced
1/4 pound small, fresh tender green beans
1 pound dry or 1 load fresh linguine
3/4 to 1 cup Classic Basil Pesto (page 17)
freshly grated parmesan cheese**

Bring a large pot of salted water to the boil. Add the diced potato to the boiling water. Cook for 5 minutes. Add the green beans and pasta to the potatoes cooking in boiling water. If you are using fresh pasta, give the green beans about 5 minutes to cook before you add the pasta. Cook all until pasta is al dente, at which time the vegetables should be properly cooked.

While the pasta is cooking, place the pesto in a shallow serving bowl. Drain pasta, reserving some pasta water. Transfer the cooked pasta, green beans, and potato to the serving bowl containing the pesto, and toss. Add 1 to 2 tablespoons of cooking water, if necessary, to enable the pesto to coat the pasta. Serve with freshly grated Parmesan. Serves 4 to 6.

Pesto Marinara Sauce with Lobster

1/4 cup olive oil
1 cup chopped onions
2 cloves garlic, finely minced
1 (2 pound-3 ounce) can plum tomatoes,
undrained, mashed with a fork to a pulp
2/3 cup Oregano Pesto (page 32)
6 (5 ounces each) frozen rock lobster tails, thawed
1 pound of dry or1 load of fresh spaghetti
freshly grated Parmesan cheese

To make sauce, sauté onions and garlic in hot oil until tender, but not brown, in large saucepan. Add tomatoes, stir and let come to a boil. Lower heat and simmer gently for 30 minutes. Add Pesto. Cook for another 5 minutes. Meanwhile, cut under-shells of lobsters lengthwise, leaving top shell intact. Remove lobster meat whole and wash thoroughly. Add lobster meat to sauce. Simmer for about 20 minutes, covered.

Meanwhile cook spaghetti until al dente, drain, and arrange in center of a heated serving platter. Remove lobster tails from sauce then pour sauce over cooked spaghetti. Sprinkle with Parmesan cheese. Arrange lobster meat around spaghetti with sauce. Serve immediately. Serves 4 to 6.

Angel Hair with Purple Pesto

The sun-dried tomatoes add a little texture and color to this creamy sauce.

1/2 cup Purple Pesto (page 19)
1 pound dry or fresh angel hair pasta
1/4 cup heavy cream
1 cup minced smoked turkey or chicken
freshly grated Parmesan cheese
very finely slivered sun-dried tomatoes for garnish

Place pesto in a large serving bowl.

Meanwhile, cook the angel hair until al dente, or firm to the bite. Stir the cream and 1 tablespoon of the hot pasta water into the pesto. Drain the pasta and transfer it to the serving bowl. Toss with the pesto and smoked turkey. Serve garnished with freshly grated Parmesan cheese and slivered sun-dried tomatoes. Serves 4.

Garlic Pesto Snow Peas with Pasta

The crunchy, sweet flavor of snow peas with the bite of garlic makes this dish a favorite over any pasta. Try adding a little crab or shrimp for more flavor.

1 pound dry or 1 load fresh pasta
3/4 pound fresh snow peas
OR young sugar snap peas
2 tablespoons butter
1/4 cup Garlic Chive Pesto (page 36)
OR Garlic Thyme Pesto (page 39)
1 cup thinly sliced scallions
1 pint half and half
salt and freshly ground pepper to taste
freshly grated Parmesan cheese

Wash and string the peas. Cut on the diagonal into 1/2-inch pieces. You should have about 3 cups.

In a large pan, melt the butter with half of the pesto. Add the peas and scallions and sauté over a low heat until tender, 8 to 10 minutes. Add the cream, and salt and pepper to taste. Reduce until the sauce is slightly thickened, about 2 minutes. Stir in the remaining pesto. Taste and adjust for seasoning. Toss with hot pasta and serve with freshly grated Parmesan. Serves 4.

Lemon Pesto Shellfish Sauce

1/3 cup olive oil
1/2 pound fresh scallops
1 garlic clove, crushed
2 shallots, finely chopped
1/2 pound medium-size peeled and deveined shrimp
2/3 cup dry white wine
salt and freshly ground black pepper to taste
1 (8-ounce) can clams, drained
1/2 cup Lemon Thyme Pesto (page 40)
2 tablespoons chopped fresh parsley

In a frying pan, heat 3 tablespoons of olive oil. Add scallops. Sauté for about 4 minutes. Heat remaining oil in a medium-size saucepan. Add garlic, shallots and shrimp. Cook until shallots are soft and shrimp turns pink. Remove shrimp and set aside.Meanwhile cook pasta until al dente, drain, and set aside.

Add white wine to shallots and garlic. Bring to a boil. Simmer gently, uncovered, until reduced slightly. Add clams and Lemon Thyme Pesto and simmer for several more minutes. Season with salt and pepper to taste. Add scallops and shrimp. Gently toss with hot pasta. Garnish with fresh parsley. Serves 4.

Fennel and Sun-Dried Tomato Sauce

Serve this mildly licorice flavored sauce over your favorite pasta.

*1/4 cup olive oil
2 tablespoons minced onion
1 (14 ounce) can Italian-style plum tomatoes
with juice, chopped
1/2 cup Fennel Pesto (page 26)
1/4 cup minced, drained, and
blotted sun-dried tomatoes, packed in oil
2 tablespoons fennel tops, finely chopped
(fernlike tops saved from fennel)
salt and freshly ground black pepper to taste*

Heat the oil in a medium skillet. Add the onion. Sauté, stirring, over low heat until the onion is soft but not browned, about 3 minutes. Add the plum tomatoes and pesto; cook, stirring and crushing tomatoes, with the side of a spoon, until juices are slightly reduced and the sauce is thickened, about 15 minutes. Add the sun-dried tomatoes and fennel tops. Simmer over low heat 5 minutes. Season with salt and pepper to taste. Toss with hot pasta. Serves 4.

Red Ravioli al Pesto

These tomato-pink raviolis have a pretty pastel green filling. Boil them in chicken broth and serve in soup dishes.

FILLING

2 cups ricotta cheese
1/4 cup Classic Basil Pesto (page 17)
1 egg yolk
salt and freshly ground white pepper to taste

1 pound or 1 full load fresh tomato pasta
3 quarts chicken broth
freshly grated Parmesan cheese
Italian flat-parsley leaves, chopped

To make the filling, put the ricotta in a sieve for 3 to 4 hours to drain off any excess liquid. It should be as dry as possible for the filling. In a bowl, combine the ricotta, pesto, egg yolk, and salt and pepper, forming an even mixture. Set it aside in the refrigerator, covered, until you are ready to use it.

Roll out fresh tomato pasta dough into 2-inch by 8-inch strips about 1/16-inch thick. Working with one strip of dough at a time, space little mounds of filling (generous 1/2 teaspoonfuls) 2 inches apart in rows on the strip of pasta. With your fingers, moisten the dough around each mound of filling

with a little water. Place a second sheet of dough on top of the first and with your hands, press firmly all around the mounds of filling to seal the sheets together. With a knife or, preferably, a fluted-edged pastry wheel, cut each ravioli strip into four 2-inch by 2-inch raviolis. Press down all around the edges of each ravioli while the dough is still very soft to assure that each is well sealed. Work very quickly to prevent the dough from drying out.

Bring the broth to a boil, drop in the ravioli and cook about 3 minutes. Remember that they will continue to cook in the hot broth off the heat. Serve in flat soup dishes garnished with parsley and pass with freshly grated Parmesan. Serves 4 to 6.

Summer Savory Carrot Sauce

This sauce is very pretty served over spinach fettuccine.

**1 pound dry or 1 load of fresh pasta
1/4 cup butter
1-1/2 cups finely diced baby carrots
2/3 cup finely diced scallions
1-1/2 cups finely diced ripe plum tomatoes, drained
1/3 cup Summer Savory Pesto (page 38)
About 1/2 cup heavy cream
salt and freshly ground pepper to taste
1/4 teaspoon lemon juice or to taste
Italian flat-leaf parsley, chopped**

Melt the butter in a large sauté pan, and sauté the carrots slowly for 2 or 3 minutes, being careful not to brown them. Add the scallions and continue sautéing for 2 minutes. Add the tomatoes and sauté briefly.

With a fork, gently stir in the pesto, leaving small green pieces. Add the cream over the vegetables. Season with salt and pepper to taste. Simmer very briefly, for 1 to 2 minutes, to reduce sauce. Stir the sauce as little as possible to retain the texture of the tomatoes and pesto. Add lemon juice to taste. Serve over hot pasta and garnish with parsley. Serves 4.

Tarragon Cream Salmon with Pasta

Smoked salmon is always a treat and this delicate sauce brings out its flavor.

1 pound dry or 1 load of fresh fettuccine
3 tablespoons butter
6 tablespoons thinly sliced shallots
1-1/2 cups heavy cream
freshly ground pepper to taste
1/3 cup Tarragon Cream Pesto (page 44)
1/2 pound smoked Norwegian salmon,
julienne-sliced in 1/4-inch strips
fresh tarragon sprigs for garnish

In a saucepan, melt 2 tablespoons of the butter. Sauté the shallots over low heat for 2 to 3 minutes. Add the cream and freshly ground pepper and continue to simmer until the cream is reduced to about half. Meanwhile, cook pasta until al dente. Drain, return to the warm pan and toss with the remaining 1 tablespoon of butter.

When the cream is reduced, stir in the pesto and the sliced smoked salmon.

Divide the pasta among 6 warm plates and spoon the salmon cream sauce over the noodles. Garnish with fresh tarragon sprigs. Serves 4 to 6.

71

Tuna and Parsley Pesto Sauce

This nutritious, easy-to-make sauce goes well with penne or spaghetti.

1/2 cup Parsley Pesto Sauce (page 30)
2 (6-1/2 ounce) cans imported Italian tuna
packed in olive oil
1 pound dry or 1 load of fresh pasta
1/2 cup black olives, chopped
freshly grated Parmesan cheese

Place pesto in a large serving bowl and add drained tuna.

Meanwhile, cook the pasta until al dente, or firm to the bite. With a ladle, carefully remove 1/4 cup of the pasta cooking liquid; add to pesto. Drain pasta. Add immediately to pesto and tuna. Stir to coat. Stir in the olives and serve. Pass with freshly grated Parmesan cheese. Serves 4 to 6.

Tomato Anchovy Pesto Pasta Sauce

This unusual sauce is made with salt-cured olives that are cultivated along the Mediterranean, picked fully ripe and cured dry with salt. You can find them at many grocery store delis.

1 pound dry or 1 load fresh pasta
1-1/2 tablespoons butter
1-1/2 cups Spanish onion, thinly sliced
and quartered
1/4 cup Herbed Anchovy Pesto (page 45) or to taste
3 cups sliced peeled ripe plum tomatoes
1/4 cup thinly sliced salt-cured dry black olives
freshly ground pepper to taste

Melt the butter in a large sauté pan. Sauté the onion very slowly for about 10 minutes. Be sure not to brown. Add pesto, tomatoes, and olives. Simmer gently, stirring occasionally, for about 10 minutes, until the liquids are reduced slightly.

Meanwhile, cook pasta until al dente, drain, and transfer to a heated serving bowl. Season sauce to taste with freshly ground pepper, toss with pasta, and serve. Serves 4.

Fusilli with Sausage and Caraway Pesto Cream Sauce

1 pound dry or 1 full load of fresh fusilli
1/4 cup butter
1-1/2 pounds sweet Italian sausage,
casings removed
2 cups heavy cream
1/2 cup Caraway Thyme Pesto (page 41)
3/4 cup dry white wine
1 tablespoon minced fresh parsley
1/2 teaspoon nutmeg
1 cup freshly grated Parmesan cheese
1 tablespoon minced fresh parsley

In large skillet, melt butter. Stir in sausage and fry until brown. Remove sausage and drain grease. Return sausage to skillet and stir in cream, wine, pesto, 1 tablespoon parsley, nutmeg and 1/2 cup Parmesan cheese. Simmer for 3-4 minutes.

Cook fusilli until al dente, drain, and transfer to a heated serving platter. Stir in 2 tablespoons of sausage mixture and remaining 1/2 cup Parmesan cheese. Toss until pasta is coated. Pour remaining sausage mixture over pasta. Sprinkle with 1 tablespoon parsley and serve immediately. Serves 4 to 6.

Chapter 3

On the
Side

Minted Pesto Butter

Basil Mint Pesto can be made when basil is plentiful, then frozen and used as required. Treat yourself to hot vegetables drenched in this special butter in mid-winter to remind you of balmy summer days. Or use with breadsticks or to spread on crusty Italian or French bread. Of course, you can can easily create as many pesto butters as there are pestos. So let your imagination go and come up with your own combinations to give any meal an Italian accent.

1/4 cup Basil Mint Pesto (page 18)
1/2 cup butter or margarine, room temperature

Blend pesto and butter in a small ceramic bowl until well combined. Makes 2/3 cup.

Spaghetti Squash with Basil Lime Pesto

Spaghetti squash has a pulp that naturally separates into strands. It makes a great stand-in for linguini or spaghetti.

1 spaghetti squash (2 to 3 pounds)
2/3 cup Basil Lime Pesto (page 34)
1/2 cup freshly grated Parmesan cheese
salt and freshly ground black pepper to taste

Oven: Preheat oven to 350°. Pierce squash in several places with a fork and place in a rimmed baking pan. Bake, uncovered until shell gives when pressed, about 1-1/4 to 1-1/2 hours. Cut baked squash in half; scrape out and discard seeds.

Microwave: Cut squash in half lengthwise and scrape out and discard seeds. Place halves, open side up, in a 9 x 13-inch microwave dish. Cover with plastic food wrap. Cook on highest setting for 15 to 20 minutes, or until tender. Let stand, covered, for an additional 5 minutes.

Loosen squash strands with a fork and scoop out into a warm serving bowl. Add the pesto and mix lightly, using 2 forks. Pass with Parmesan cheese. Serves 4 to 6.

Pesto Vegetables

This flavorful vegetarian sauce makes a light and healthy addition to any meal. Try spooning it over rice for a wonderful side dish.

*2 tablespoons olive oil
1 large onion, coarsely chopped
1 green pepper, cubed (1-inch pieces)
3/4 cup mushrooms, sliced
1 garlic clove, minced
1/2 pound cherry tomatoes, halved
1/4 cup chopped fresh parsley
1/3 cup chopped black olives
1/2 cup fresh lemon juice
1/4 cup dry red wine
3 tablespoons Pistachio Basil Pesto (page 25)
freshly grated Parmesan cheese*

Heat the oil over medium high heat in a large saucepan. Add the onion, green pepper, mushrooms, and garlic. Sauté for 5 minutes, or until the vegetables are just tender.

Add the remaining ingredients and stir until well blended. Cook, partially covered, for 10 minutes. Serve over hot rice or pasta (a short pasta, such as ziti, penne, fusilli, or farfelle is recommended). Pass freshly grated parmesan cheese. Serves 4 to 6.

Chilled Cilantro Lobster

This mouth watering salad goes great with crusty French bread and a glass of Chardonnay.

1 bay leaf, crumbled
3 or 4 lemon slices, halved
1/4 teaspoon salt
2 large lobster tails
3 tablespoons Cilantro Pesto (page 33)
3 tablespoons sour cream
3 tablespoons mayonnaise
1 teaspoon lime juice
salt and freshly ground white pepper to taste
Romaine lettuce leaves
1 ripe avocado, sliced
lime slices and fresh cilantro sprigs for garnish

Bring 3 quarts of water with bay leaf, lemon slices, and salt to a boil. Add lobster to boiling water. Simmer, covered, for 5 to 8 minutes, until tails are cooked through. Remove lobster with a slotted spoon. Allow to cool. Slit the underside and remove meat. Cut into bite-sized chunks and refrigerate.

Combine the pesto, sour cream, mayonnaise, and lime juice in a small bowl. Add salt and pepper to taste. Arrange the lobster and avocado slices on the lettuce. Pour the cilantro sauce over the shrimp and garnish with lime and cilantro. Serves 2.

Shrimp with Tarragon Cream Fraîche

This dish is made with Creme Fraîche, a versatile thickening agent you need to make a least 24 hours ahead. It is delicious with fresh fruit and will keep for a week or longer, just add more cream to continue the culture.

CREME FRAICHE

1 cup heavy cream
1 teaspoon buttermilk

1/4 cup Tarragon Cream Pesto (page 44)
1/3 cup Creme Fraîche
lemon juice and salt to taste
Butter lettuce leaves
1/2 pound medium-sized cooked shrimp
lemon wedges and fresh tarragon sprigs for garnish

Combine the cream and buttermilk in a covered glass jar. Let stand at room temperature until thickened, about 24 hours, then refrigerate.

Combine the pesto and Creme Fraîche with a little lemon juice and salt to taste. Arrange lettuce leaves topped with shrimp on individual serving plates. Spoon pesto sauce over the shrimp and garnish with lemon wedges and tarragon sprigs. Serves 2 to 4.

Purple Pesto Ceviche

Use only the freshest seafood in this variation of the traditional Mexican Ceviche. The fish stays tender because the fruit acids in the lime juice do the "cooking." Try using a combination of shrimp and scallops.

1 pound bay shrimp OR scallops
1 teaspoon salt
3/4 cup fresh lime juice
1/3 cup minced scallions
1/4 cup Purple Basil Pesto (page 19)
1/2 teaspoon crushed chili peppers
l teaspoon dried oregano OR
1 tablespoon minced fresh oregano
1 large bay leaf, crumbled
1/4 cup olive oil
1/4 cup sliced stuffed olives
1 cup diced and seeded ripe tomatoes
1/4 cup minced Italian flat parsley

Place the shrimp or scallops in a ceramic bowl. Add the salt, lime juice, and scallions. Stir to combine gently and refrigerate for at least 3 to 4 hours, preferably overnight.

Drain shrimp or scallops, reserving 1/2 cup of the marinade. Combine the 1/2 cup marinade with the pesto, chili peppers, oregano, bay leaf, and olive oil. Add to the scallops along with the olives, tomatoes, and parsley. Serve cold. Serves 4 to 6.

Zucchini Pesto Soup

Zucchini is one of Italy's best-loved and most abundant vegetables. Here, it is presented as a purée brightened with pesto. It is best served fresh, but can be reheated.

3 pounds medium size zucchini
3 tablespoons olive oil
2 medium onions, chopped
6 cups chicken broth
3/4 cup Classic Basil Pesto (page 17)
1/3 cup coarsely grated Parmesan cheese
fresh basil sprigs (optional)

Coarsely grate one zucchini and refrigerate. Slice remaining zucchini into thin, crosswise slices. Heat oil in a 5 to 6 quart saucepan, over medium-high heat. Add onions, and cook, stirring often, until onions become translucent, about 10 minutes. Add sliced zucchini and one cup of broth. Bring to a boil over a high heat, reduce heat, cover, and simmer until zucchini is tender, about 15 minutes.

In a blender or food processor, purée cooked zucchini mixture until it reaches a smooth consistency. Return to pan and stir in remaining broth. Heat until the mixture just boils, remove from heat and stir in pesto.

Ladle into bowls and garnish with remaining zucchini and fresh basil sprigs. Pass with freshly grated Parmesan. Serves 6 to 8.

Ricotta Basil Pesto Cucumber Soup

This unusual soup is served cold and makes a fine addition to a summer luncheon menu. Use long, seedless cucumbers to make the preparation easier.

2 cups peeled, seeded, and diced cucumber
1/2 cup Ricotta Basil Pesto (page 23)
1 small garlic clove, pressed
1-1/2 cups yogurt
1/2 cup sour cream
2 tablespoons rice OR white vinegar
salt and freshly ground white pepper to taste
fresh parsley sprig for garnish

Combine the cucumber, pesto, garlic, yogurt, sour cream, vinegar, and salt in a food processor or blender. Blend until smooth. Taste, add white pepper, and adjust the seasoning. Pour into a ceramic bowl, cover and chill in the refrigerator for up to 4 hours before serving. Serve very cold, garnished with parsley. Serves 4.

Minestrone alia Genovese

In Italy, minestrone means literally, "big soup". It implies that every bowl is full of vegetables, grains, beans, and herbs. The addition of delicious pesto makes it even bigger.

1 cup Classic Basil Pesto (page 17)
2 large leeks
3 quarts chicken broth
2 large carrots, peeled and coarsely chopped
3 stalks celery, thinly sliced
2 (15 ounce) cans cannellini beans,
drained and rinsed
2 cups dry elbow macaroni
1 pound yellow zucchini, cut into 1/2-inch chunks
1 large red bell pepper, seeded and chopped
1 cup frozen tiny peas, thawed

Trim ends and tops from leeks. Split lengthwise, rinse, and slice crosswise. In an 8 quart pan, combine leeks, broth, carrots, and celery; bring to a boil. Reduce heat, cover, and simmer until vegetables are tender about 15 minutes. Add beans, macaroni, squash, and bell pepper; cover and simmer until macaroni is tender about 10 minutes. Add peas and bring to a boil. Stir in 1/2 cup of pesto. Serve hot or chilled. Pass with remaining pesto to season soup to taste. Serves 8 to 10.

Vegetable Sorrel Soup

The fresh, mildly lemon flavor of fresh sorrel livens up this soup which can be served hot as a first course or cold with a light luncheon.

3 tablespoons butter
5 scallions, chopped (tops included)
1 cup grated, unpeeled zucchini
1 cup grated, peeled carrot
3/4 cup Basil Sorrel Pesto (page 21)
4 cups chicken broth
salt and freshly ground black pepper to taste

Melt the butter in a large saucepan and sauté the onion, zucchini, and carrot for 4 to 5 minutes, until just tender. Do not brown. Add the pesto and 3 cups of the chicken broth. Bring to a simmer and remove from the heat.

Purée the soup in a food processor or blender. Return to the saucepan and add the remaining 1 cup chicken broth. Season to taste with salt and freshly ground pepper. Serves 4.

Herb Bouquet Soup with Mussels

Serve this soup with crusty garlic bread and garnish with fresh parsley. The recipe can be varied to your taste and imagination. Substitute scallops, clams, or shrimp. You can also vary the recipe by adding Summer Savory, Garlic Thyme or Basil Watercress Pesto instead of Herb Bouquet.

3 pounds mussels in their shells
2 large garlic cloves, minced
1 small onion, chopped
1 bay leaf, crumbled
1 cup dry red wine
1 cup water
1/4 cup olive oil
6 to 8 large scallions, chopped (some tops)
3 tomatoes, chopped
OR 1-1/2 cups canned Italian plum tomatoes
1/2 cup tomato puree
2 tablespoons Herb Bouquet Pesto (page 37)
salt and freshly ground pepper to taste
chopped fresh parsley for garnish

Scrub the mussels well and remove the stringy beard with a knife. A soapless scouring pad works well for scrubbing. Discard any mussels that are open. Mussels must be very fresh and used within

one day of purchase.

In a large saucepan, combine the mussels, garlic, onion, bay leaf, wine and water. Shake to distribute the mussels and steam for about 3 to 4 minutes, just until the mussels open. Remove the opened mussels, discarding any that are closed. Strain the broth through 2 thicknesses of dampened cheese cloth and set aside.

Heat the olive oil in a large heavy skillet, and sauté the scallions until softened. Add the strained mussel broth slowly, leaving any remaining sediment in the pan. Cook rapidly for 4 or 5 minutes to reduce the volume and intensify the flavor. Add the remaining ingredients and simmer for about 5 minutes. Remove the mussels from the shells and add to the soup and taste for seasoning. Sprinkle a little chopped parsley to garnish each soup bowl. Serves 4.

Minestrone Verde

This soup is almost pastoral in its green color, with the delightful flavors of fresh vegetables and herbs. Add the pesto sauce right before serving. The pesto's flavor and aroma are released when you put it into the hot soup.

2 to 3 leeks
1/4 cup extra-virgin olive oil
2-3 garlic cloves, peeled and minced
1 onion, peeled and thinly sliced
1/2 cabbage, finely shredded
1/2 pound fresh early green beans
3-4 small, firm zucchini, trimmed and sliced
handful chopped Italian parsley
5-10 leaves fresh basil, coarsely chopped
3/4 cup imported conchigliette
2 cups fresh or frozen peas
salt and freshly ground black pepper to taste
1 cup Basil & Oregano Pesto (page 22)
freshly grated Parmesan cheese

Make two vertical cuts lengthwise in the leeks to expose the layers, and wash thoroughly under cold running water. Drain and coarsely chop. Heat the extra-virgin olive oil in a soup pot. Add the garlic, onion, and leeks. Cook over moderate heat for 2 minutes, stirring frequently. Add the cabbage, stir, and cover pan. Cook covered until cabbage begins

to wilt. Add water to cover by 2 inches and bring to a boil. Turn the heat down and simmer until cabbage is tender. Add the green beans, zucchini, parsley, and basil and simmer until vegetables are barely done. Add the pasta and continue cooking until it is al dente. Add the peas at the last minute. Add salt and pepper to taste. Before serving, stir 1 teaspoon of pesto into each individual soup bowl. Serve immediately or at room temperature. Pass extra pesto and Parmesan cheese. Serves 6 to 8.

Pesto Chicken and Pasta Salad

This is a quick and light addition to lunch or served on lettuce before a main course.

**1 pound dry or 1 load fresh penne
or other tubular pasta
1 cup French Tarragon Pesto (page 43)
3 cups shredded cooked chicken
1 container cherry tomatoes, rinsed and stemmed
1/4 cup pitted brine-cured black olives
1/2 cup broken walnuts**

Cook the pasta until al dente and drain. Rinse with cool water and drain again.

Toss the pasta with the French Tarragon Pesto, chicken, tomatoes, and olives. Add the broken walnuts just before serving. Serve at room temperature. Serves 6 to 8.

Tortellini, Shrimp & Pesto Salad

Here's a salad that's perfect for picnics and potlucks. You can make it the night before, then refrigerate it to let the flavors blend. Both fresh and dry tortellini work well in this recipe.

1 cup Classic Basil Pesto (page 17)
1/4 cup plus 1 tablespoon red wine vinegar
1 pound fresh tortellini
1 medium-size red bell pepper,
seeded and cut into thin bite-size strips
1/2 pound bay shrimp

To make dressing, thoroughly blend red wine vinegar with Classic Basil Pesto and set aside. Cook tortellini until al dente. Drain, rinse with cold water, and drain well again.

In a large ceramic bowl, lightly mix the tortellini,pesto dressing, bell pepper strips, and shrimp. Cover mixture and refrigerate for at least 1 hour or up to 8 hours. Serves 4 to 6.

Fennel Fruit Salad

Prepare the ingredients for the salad ahead of time and let them chill in the refrigerator.

About 2 cups romaine lettuce OR red leaf lettuce
1 large navel orange, peeled and sectioned
1 sweet ruby red grapefruit, peeled and sectioned
1 cup coarsely chopped celery
1/2 cup walnut halves for garnish
3 tablespoons Fennel Pesto (page 26)
1 tablespoon lemon juice
2 tablespoons walnut oil
salt to taste
2 medium-size ripe avocados, peeled and sliced
green seedless grapes for garnish

Wash and dry the lettuce leaves. Cut orange and grapefruit into bite-sized pieces and set aside. Cook celery in microwave in 2 cups of water on high for 3 minutes then drain. Cover lettuce, orange, grapefruit, and celery with plastic wrap and chill in the refrigerator. Meanwhile, toast the walnuts in a 325°F. oven about 10 minutes, until light brown.

Blend together the pesto, lemon juice, and walnut oil. Add salt to taste and chill. When ready to serve, tear lettuce into bite-sized pieces and place in a large bowl. Add remaining ingredients and toss. Place salad on individual salad plates, drizzle with dressing and garnish with walnuts and grapes. Serves 4.

Cilantro Pesto Pasta Salad

Cilantro pesto is a regional American version of the Italian basil pesto.

1/2 pound dry wagon wheels or fusilli
1 tablespoon virgin olive oil
2 medium-size firm tomatoes
2/3 cup Cilantro Pesto (page 33)
fresh cilantro leaves and pine nuts for garnish

Cook the pasta in boiling water until al dente, rinse in cold water, and drain. Transfer to a mixing bowl and toss with 1 tablespoon olive oil.

Score, then blanch the tomatoes in boiling water for 30 seconds to loosen the skins. Peel, halve, and seed under running water. Pat dry and chop into 1/4-inch pieces.

Add the pesto to the pasta and mix thoroughly. If it is too dry, add a few drops of oil. Transfer to a serving dish. Gently fold in the tomatoes before serving. Garnish the salad with sprigs of fresh cilantro and some pine nuts. Serves 4.

Continental Potato Salad

This crunchy potato salad makes a great picnic lunch with a cold white zinfandel.

3 tablespoons Tarragon Cream Pesto (page 44)
2 tablespoons country dijon mustard
1 tablespoon tarragon vinegar
1/2 cup mayonnaise
salt and freshly ground black pepper to taste
1 cup cooked, shredded chicken breast (skinless)
2 cups quartered, sliced new potatoes
2 cups fresh green beans, cut in l-inch pieces
1/2 cup walnuts, coarsely chopped
1/2 cup sliced mushrooms
1/2 cup apple, coarsely chopped
butter lettuce
fresh tomato slices for garnish

Steam the new potatoes and green beans in a vegetable steamer over boiling water until just tender, about 10 minutes. Allow to chill in the refrigerator.

Whisk together the pesto, mustard, vinegar, and mayonnaise. Season to taste with salt and freshly ground pepper and allow to chill.

Mix together chicken, potatoes and beans. Fold in the dressing along with the remaining ingredients. Spoon the salad onto a bed of lettuce and garnish with fresh sliced tomato. Serve cold. Serves 4.

Red Ricotta Caraway Coleslaw

This creamy thyme-based pesto adds a slightly sweet flavor to this colorful slaw made of red cabbage.

3 tablespoons Ricotta Caraway
Thyme Pesto (page 42)
2 tablespoons white vinegar
2 tablespoons mayonnaise
1/2 teaspoon sugar
1/4 teaspoon salt
2 cups grated carrots
3 cups grated red cabbage
2 to 3 tablespoons minced scallions,
including some green
leaf lettuce
1 (8 ounce) can Mandarin oranges for garnish

In a ceramic bowl, whisk together the pesto, vinegar, mayonnaise, sugar, and salt to make the dressing. Toss the carrots, cabbage, and scallions with the dressing and taste for seasoning. Chill.

Arrange the lettuce on individual salad plates. Top with the coleslaw and garnish with Mandarin oranges. Serve cold. Serves 4 to 6.

Warm Feta Cheese Salad

Dip feta cheese chunks in pesto, coat with bread crumbs, and toast lightly. The resulting "croutons" have a warm cheese center with a crunchy outside. They make a delicious topping for the cold mixed greens and tangy, walnut vinaigrette dressing.

1/2 cup roughly chopped walnuts
1/2 pound feta cheese
1/2 cup Classic Basil Pesto (page 17)
or Herb Bouquet Pesto (page 37)
1 cup fine dry bread crumbs
2 tablespoons dijon mustard
2 tablespoons tarragon vinegar
1/3 cup walnut oil
salt and freshly ground pepper
1/2 small sweet yellow pepper, julienne sliced
mixed salad greens (oak leaf and red leaf lettuces,
Belgian endive, watercress, or spinach)
red seedless grapes for garnish

Preheat the oven to 300 °F. Toast the walnuts in the oven for about 10 minutes to bring out the natural oils. Set aside and reset oven to 450 °F.

Slice the feta cheese into slices about 1/2-inch thick then cut into medium-sized chunks. Dip the cheese in the pesto, coating all sides. Then coat with dry bread crumbs all sides and place on a lightly oiled baking dish.

In a ceramic bowl, whisk together the mustard, vinegar, and the walnut oil. Season with salt and freshly ground pepper. Add the warm toasted walnuts. Taste for seasoning.

Meanwhile, bake the cheese for 8 to 10 minutes, until light brown and slightly crusty on the outside.

Toss the greens, pepper, and dressing together. Place on individual salad plates, top with warm feta "croutons" and garnish with grapes. Serve at once. Serves 6.

Tuna Green Bean Bouquet

*The fresh tuna and crunchy green beans are enhanced
by the savory pesto marinade.*

*1 pound fresh tuna fillet, 1 inch thick
2 tablespoons minced red onion
1/3 cup Herb Bouquet Pesto (page 37)
6 tablespoons lemon juice
6 tablespoons olive oil
1 cup sliced fresh green beans, cut in 1/2-inch pieces
1 tablespoon finely julienned sun-dried tomatoes
1 pound freshly cooked rotini, drained and chilled
salt and freshly ground pepper to taste
sliced plum tomatoes for garnish*

Slice the fresh tuna horizontally to 1/2 inch thickness. Then slice in thin slices, about 1/4 inch wide.
Place in a ceramic dish with the red onion. For
marinade, whisk together pesto, lemon juice, and
olive oil. Pour over the tuna and onion .and marinate in the refrigerator for one half hour.

Heat a large sauté pan. Place tuna in a single
layer in the hot pan. Sauté briefly, until the fish
flakes, about 2 or 3 minutes. Remove from the
heat and cover with any remaining marinade.
Blanch beans, until just crunchy. Drain. Gently
combine tuna, beans, and tomatoes with the pasta
in a large serving bowl. Salt and pepper to taste.
Chill, and serve cold. Garnish with sliced ripe
plum tomatoes. Serves 4.

Pasta Seafood Salad

1 pound dry or 1 full load of fresh fusilli
1 pound bay scallops
2-1/2 cups clam juice
1/4 cup Herbed Anchovy Pesto (page 45)
1/4 cup virgin olive oil
2 teaspoons wine vinegar
juice of one fresh lemon
1/2 pound fresh crab meat (leg meat preferable)
1 tablespoon minced red onion
2 cups diced, peeled ripe tomatoes, well-drained
1/2 cup chopped fresh parsley leaves
leaf lettuce
freshly grated Parmesan cheese
lemon wedges

Cook the pasta until it is al dente. Drain thoroughly, toss with a small amount of olive oil and set aside. To make dressing, whisk together Herbed Anchovy Pesto, olive oil, vinegar, and lemon juice.

Rinse the scallops. Bring the clam juice to a simmer. Add the scallops and poach for 3-4 minutes, until just cooked. Drain the scallops and allow to cool in the refrigerator. Rinse crab meat in cold water and drain. Add the scallops, crab meat, red onion, tomatoes, and parsley to the pasta. Combine with the Herbed Anchovy Dressing and toss gently. Serve cold on a bed of leaf lettuce and garnish with lemon wedges. Serves 6 to 8.

Herbed Anchovy
Pasta Salad

The strong flavor of anchovies spices up the fresh, flavor of crunchy vegetables in this salad that can be served cold or at room temperature.

1/2 pound each dry medium and small shells
1 cup coarsely chopped broccoli florets
1/2 cup chopped scallions OR red onion
3/4 cup julienne-sliced carrots
3/4 cup roasted red peppers, coarsely chopped
1 cup Herbed Anchovy Pesto (page 45)
1/4 cup extra-virgin olive oil
2 tablespoons lemon juice
1/3 cup wine vinegar
fresh basil or chopped walnuts for garnish

Cook the shells until al dente. Rinse in cold water and drain. Place in a large ceramic serving bowl and set aside.

To make dressing, whisk together pesto, oil, lemon juice, and vinegar. Meanwhile, cook broccoli in the microwave on high, covered with plastic wrap, for 1 minute. Add broccoli, onions, carrots, and peppers to the pasta and mix gently. Stir in dressing and mix. Garnish with fresh basil leaves or nuts and serve immediately. Serves 6 to 8.

Pea Pods, Shrimp, and Barley Salad

The barley adds an unusual texture to this cold salad with a slightly creamy dressing. Serve with garlic toast.

1-1/4 cups uncooked pearl barley
1/2 cup broken walnuts, lightly toasted
1/2 cup Tarragon Cream Pesto (page 44)
1 tablespoon dijon mustard
2 tablespoons tarragon vinegar
1/3 cup fresh lemon juice
2 tablespoons olive oil
salt and freshly ground pepper to taste
1/4 cup sliced scallions, including some green tops
1 cup diced celery
2 pounds peeled and deveined shrimp, cooked
2 cups diced ripe tomatoes
2 cups diagonally chopped snow pea pods, steamed
crumbled feta cheese for garnish

Bring a quart of water to a boil and add the barley. Cover and simmer for 30 minutes, until the barley is just tender. Drain and rinse with cold water.

For dressing, whisk together pesto, mustard, vinegar, lemon juice, olive oil, salt, and pepper. Combine the barley, scallions, celery, walnuts, shrimp, and dressing. Fold in the tomatoes and pea pods. Chill. Garnish with feta. Serves 6 to 8.

Steamed Asparagus with Pesto Hollandaise

Hollandaise is a popular sauce for steamed asparagus. This green version can be used over any fresh vegetable in season or to make an interesting variation on the Sunday brunch classic – Eggs Benedict.

3 egg yolks
1-1/2 tablespoons fresh lemon juice
1/8 teaspoon salt
1/4 cup melted butter
1/4 cup Classic Basil Pesto (page 17)
1 pound of fresh asparagus

Whisk together egg yolks, lemon juice, and salt. Melt the butter in a double boiler Add the pesto to the butter, whisking constantly. Slowly add the egg yolk mixture to the hot butter and pesto mixture. Whisk continuously until thoroughly blended. Taste and adjust for seasoning. Serve immediately over steamed asparagus. It is best to use the sauce immediately because the green color fades if the sauce is held. Makes about 3/4 cup.

Purple Stuffed Tomatoes

This appetizer is a healthy and colorful party pleaser.

**30 to 40 ripe cherry tomatoes
1/4 cup cream cheese, at room temperature
1/4 cup ricotta cheese
1/4 cup Purple Basil Pesto (page 19)
1 tablespoon minced scallions
1 teaspoon lemon juice
salt and cayenne pepper to taste
opal basil for garnish**

Wash the tomatoes and slice the top off of each stem end. Empty out the seeds and drain upside down on paper towel.

Combine the cream cheese, ricotta, pesto, scallions, and lemon juice. Season to taste with salt and cayenne. Spoon filling into the tomato shells and chill. Arrange on a platter and garnish with sprigs of opal basil leaves. Serves 8 to 10.

Pesto Stuffed Mushrooms

These mushrooms can be an appetizer or feast on them served with a mixed green salad and French bread.

18 large mushrooms
2 tablespoons butter
1/3 cup capers
2 tablespoons Garlic Chive Pesto (page 36)
2 tablespoons sherry
1/2 cup fresh bread crumbs
1/4 cup minced fresh parsley
1/4 cup grated Swiss cheese
2 tablespoons freshly grated Parmesan cheese
2 tablespoons heavy cream
salt and freshly ground pepper
3 tablespoons melted butter
1 tablespoon grated Swiss cheese
1/4 cup chopped sun-dried tomatoes

Wash mushrooms and trim bottoms of the stems. Carefully break the stems out of the caps and finely chop the stems.

Melt 2 tablespoons butter in a sauté pan, and sauté the capers and chopped mushroom stems for 3 to 4 minutes, until slightly soft.

Add the pesto and the sherry. Simmer for approximately 2 minutes, until the sherry has reduced by half. Place in a ceramic mixing bowl and allow to cool for 5 minutes.

Add the fresh bread crumbs, parsley, and the cheeses to the pesto mixture. Add cream and stir gently. Season to taste with salt and pepper.

Brush the outside of the mushroom caps with melted butter and mound the stuffing lightly in the center. Place close together in a shallow baking dish. Top with the remaining 1 tablespoon grated Swiss cheese and a few pieces of sun-dried tomato and drizzle the caps with the remaining melted butter. Bake uncovered at 375 °F. for 15 minutes. Turn up oven to broil for the last 5 minutes, so tops of mushrooms get slightly brown and crunchy.

Mint Pesto Tabbouleh

This unusual dish from Syria with a distinctive mint flavor is usually served as an appetizer. Freeze Basil Mint Pesto so you can enjoy Tabbouleh in the winter months.

1-1/2 cups No. 2 dry bulgur or cracked wheat
3 tablespoons Basil Mint Pesto (page 18)
juice of 2 lemons
3 tablespoons olive oil
2 teaspoons whole-grain mustard
1/2 bunch fresh parsley leaves
1 tablespoon vinegar
5 scallions, chopped including some green
3 tablespoons crumbled feta cheese
1 cup diced peeled cucumber
1 cup diced ripe tomato
romaine lettuce leaves
fresh mint leaves for garnish

Place bulgur in a large mixing bowl and add 2 quarts of water. Let stand for about 2 hours.

Meanwhile, wash parsley in cold water, then wash in a mixture of cold water and the vinegar. Drain dry on paper towels, then chop. You should have about 1/2 cup chopped parsley. Whisk together the pesto, lemon juice, olive oil, mustard, and parsley.

Thoroughly drain the bulgur in a colander lined with cheesecloth. Then squeeze with your hands to

extract as much water as possible. Place the bulgar into a ceramic mixing bowl. Add the dressing, scallions, feta cheese, cucumber, and tomato. Mix thoroughly and refrigerate for 1 hour or more.

To serve, arrange romaine leaves on plates and spoon the tabbouleh onto each. Garnish with minced fresh mint if desired. Serves 4 to 6.

Pesto Bread

The pesto, cottage cheese, mustard, and pine nuts in this bread will fill the kitchen with a wonderful aroma as it bakes. Serve warm with big bowls of soup for a satisfying meal.

1 package dry yeast
1/4 cup warm water
1 teaspoon sugar
1 cup creamed cottage cheese, warmed
2 eggs, lightly beaten
2 tablespoons sugar
5 tablespoons Three Herb Pesto (page 31)
1 teaspoon salt
1 tablespoon dijon mustard
1/4 teaspoon baking soda
1/4 cup pine nuts, chopped
1/2 cup finely chopped fresh parsley leaves
2-3/4 cups all-purpose flour
2 tablespoon butter, melted
1/4 teaspoon salt

Dissolve yeast in warm water with 1 teaspoon sugar. Let stand 10 minutes. Combine cottage cheese with egg, sugar, pesto, salt, mustard, baking soda, 3 tablespoons chopped pine nuts, parsley and yeast mixture, stirring until well blended. Stir in flour, working dough until all flour is moistened. Beat well. If dough is too moist add a little more

flour. Cover with a damp towel and let rise in a
warm place until doubled in bulk, about 1 hour.

Punch down and turn dough into a well-greased
2-quart casserole dish. Let rise until doubled in
bulk, about 30 minutes. Bake at 375 °F. for 15 minutes; lower temperature to 300 °F. and bake for
another 25 minutes or until golden. Brush with
melted butter and sprinkle with salt and remaining 1 tablespoon of pine nuts when hot from the
oven.

Sun-dried Italian Plum Tomatoes

Once you have tasted your first sun-dried Italian plum tomatoes in a dish, you will probably want to add them to your list of flavorings. In fact, they are a necessary ingredient for making Purple Basil Pesto (page 19).

During the drying process, the natural sweetness and flavor of the ripe tomatoes are intensified. Then the tomatoes are packed with herbs and olive oil. The result is wonderful flavor, and just 2 tablespoons of the chopped tomatoes can transform an ordinary dish into something quite special. The oil in which the tomatoes are packed is also very flavorful and can be used in vegetable sautés.

Although specialty food stores and mail order food companies now sell these tomatoes, they are very expensive. A 10-1/2 ounce jar, which contains about 7 ounces of tomatoes, can cost over $10.

If you grow your own tomatoes, you will find it is well worth the effort to make your own sun-dried Italian plum tomatoes. And, by making your own, you can vary the flavors, using basil, oregano, thyme, or whatever herb combinations strike your fancy.

Despite the name, the flavor of these tomatoes is just fine if you dry the tomatoes in a dehydrator or oven. If you live in a dry, sunny climate, you can dry the tomatoes in the sun, as you dry other fruits. Then proceed with the recipe to the right. This recipe makes 3 half-pint jars.

5 pounds ripe Italian plum tomatoes
salt
olive oil to fill jars (about 1-1/4 cups)
herbs (5 or 6 fresh basil leaves, OR
2 or 3 fresh 2-inch sprigs of oregano and 2 or 3
fresh 2-inch sprigs of thyme, OR
8 peppercorns and 6 fresh 2-inch sprigs of thyme)

Select perfect ripe Italian plum tomatoes or another small fleshy tomato variety. Slice each tomato almost in half vertically and open like a book. Remove the stem end with a small V-cut and cut off any blemishes. You may dry the tomatoes in this form, or you can remove the pulp and seeds to reduce the drying time.

To dry in a dehydrator, place the open tomatoes skin side down on drying racks. Salt then lightly; this helps to draw out the moisture. Dry for 10 to 16 hours, until the tomato halves are leathery but not dry or hard. Small tomatoes will dry quicker than large ones. Check the dehydrator at intervals and remove the tomatoes individually as they reach the leathery stage.

To dry in the oven, preheat the oven to 200°F. Place the tomatoes on racks on baking sheets (probably 2 large cookie sheets will be needed). Salt the tomatoes lightly. Bake for about 6 to 7 hours. Switch the baking sheets from top to bottom after a few hours, and remove the smaller tomatoes as they dry.

Cool slightly. Fold the tomato halves closed. Pack very tightly in half-pint jars, inserting the

sprigs of fresh herbs between the tomatoes. It's easiest to pack the tomatoes upright and to make 2 layers of tomatoes with herbs in each layer. Add olive oil to completely cover the tomatoes. Poke a knife in around the edges to let any air bubbles escape. Seal the jars tightly.

Store at room temperature for 6 weeks to allow the flavors to develop.

Chapter 4

Main Courses

Pesto Vegetable Calzone

Calzone is like a pizza folded over to capture the filling. These individual calzones make great party snacks and leftovers are a superb addition to a packed lunch.

2 batches Simple Pizza Crust (page 119)
olive oil

Vegetable and Cheese Filling

2 eggplants, sliced
olive oil
1 red pepper, chopped
1 green pepper, chopped
2 zucchini, chopped
3/4 cup Three Herb Pesto (page 31)
3/4 cup grated mozzarella cheese
3 tablespoons pine nuts
salt and freshly ground black pepper to taste

To make filling, brush eggplant slices with a little olive oil and cook under a hot broiler for 3-4 minutes on each side or until golden. Drain on paper towel and chop. Turn down oven to 400°F.

Heat 1 tablespoon oil in a frying pan over a medium heat, add red pepper, green pepper, zucchini and pesto and cook, stirring, for 3 minutes or until vegetables are soft. Mix in eggplant and set aside to cool. Add cheese, pine nuts, salt and black

pepper to vegetable mixture and mix to combine.

Prepare pizza dough as described in recipe. Divide dough into eight portions and make each into a 1/4-inch thick by 6-inch diameter round shape. Place spoonfuls of filling in the center of each dough round, brush the edges with water, then fold over to form a half circle. Using a fork, press edges together, sealing and making a decorative pattern. Brush calzone with oil, place on lightly greased baking trays and bake for 20 minutes or until puffed and golden. Makes 8.

Pesto Cheese Torta with Grilled Chops

This torta is a delicious combination of two popular Italian cheeses—delicate ricotta and rich mascarpone with lively pesto and pine nuts. Serve with hot, crusty garlic bread.

> *1/2 cup Garlic Thyme Pesto (page 39)*
> *1/2 cup pine nuts*
> *1 cup whole-milk or part-skim ricotta cheese,*
> *at room temperature*
> *1 cup mascarpone or Neufchatel cheese,*
> *at room temperature*
> *salt and freshly ground pepper to taste*
> *fresh basil leaves or sprigs*
> *red bell pepper strips and zucchini spears*
> *2 tablespoons butter*
> *4 pounds of lean pork, lamb, or veal chops*

MEAT BASTING SAUCE

> *1/4 cup Rosemary Pesto (page 35)*
> *3 tablespoons olive oil*
> *1 tablespoon of minced onion*
> *2 tablespoons of lemon juice*

Spread pine nuts in a 9-inch pie pan and bake in a 350°F. oven until golden (about 7 minutes), shaking

pan occasionally. In a food processor or a large bowl, combine ricotta cheese, mascarpone, and 1/2 cup Garlic Thyme Pesto. Blend or beat with an electric mixer until smooth. Season to taste with salt, if desired. Stir in half the pine nuts.

Line a small bowl (about 2-1/2-cup capacity) with a double layer of dampened cheesecloth, leaving a 2-inch border of cloth draped over edge of bowl. Spoon in cheese mixture, fold cloth over top, and press down lightly to compact. Cover with plastic wrap and refrigerate until firm (at least 2 hours) or until next day.

When torta is ready, coat the grill with non-stick vegetable spray and preheat to medium hot. Whisk together Rosemary Pesto, olive oil, onion, and lemon juice to make basting sauce. Use a brush to coat chops with sauce. Grill the meat, basting frequently, to the desired doneness.

Melt butter in a sauté pan and cook bell pepper and zuchinni until just tender. Unfold cheesecloth from around torta and invert bowl onto the center of a large serving plate. Let torta slip out and remove cheesecloth. Sprinkle torta with remaining pine nuts. Surround with grilled chops and sauteéd vegetables and garnish with fresh basil leaves. Serves 10 to 12.

Pizzette Basil

Individual pizzas are great as a party food, and make excellent snacks or light lunches. Delicious cold as well as hot, they are great to keep in the refrigerator or freezer for emergencies.

1 batch Simple Pizza Crust (page 119)
1/2 pound ricotta cheese
2 teaspoons olive oil
1/3 cup Classic Basil Pesto (page 17)
6 scallions, diced
1/2 cup small mushrooms, sliced
2 teaspoons brown sugar
3-1/2 ounces sliced pepperoni
1 cup cherry tomatoes, quartered
1 tablespoon chopped fresh basil
1/4 pound mozzarella cheese, grated

Preheat oven to 350°F. Prepare pizza dough as described in recipe. Divide dough into four portions and shape each to form a 6-inch round. Place rounds on lightly greased baking trays and set aside.

Place ricotta cheese and pesto in a bowl and mix to combine. Spread pesto mixture over dough and bake for 10 minutes.

Meanwhile, heat oil in a frying pan over a medium heat. Add scallions, mushrooms and sugar and cook, stirring, for 4 minutes or until veg-

etables are soft. Remove pizzettes from oven and spread on scallion mixture then top with pepperoni, tomatoes and basil. Sprinkle with cheese and bake for another 20-25 minutes or until crusts are crisp.

SIMPLE PIZZA CRUST

1 teaspoon active dry yeast
pinch sugar
2/3 cup warm water
2 cups flour
1/2 teaspoon salt
1/4 cup olive oil

Place yeast, sugar, and water in a large bowl and mix to dissolve. Set aside in a warm, draft-free place for 5 minutes or until foamy.

Place flour and salt in a food processor or blender and pulse once or twice to sift. With machine running slowly pour in oil and yeast mixture and process to form a rough dough. Turn dough onto a lightly floured surface and knead for 5 minutes or until soft and shiny. Add more flour if necessary.

Lightly oil a large bowl then roll the dough around to cover the surface with oil. Cover bowl tightly with plastic wrap and place in a warm, draft-free place for 1-1/2 to 2 hours or until dough has doubled in volume. Knock down and remove dough from bowl. Knead briefly before using. Makes 1 large or 4 individual crusts.

Three Herb Pesto Pizza

This full sized tomato and pesto-topped pizza is lighter than traditional American pizzas, but it is packed with flavor just the same.

1 batch Simple Pizza Crust (page 119)
1/2 cup Three Herb Pesto (page 31)
2 tablespoons olive oil
1/4 cup sliced black olives
2 cups shredded mozzarella cheese
1 pound ripe Italian style tomatoes, cored and sliced
1 garlic clove, finely minced
salt and freshly ground black pepper to taste

Prepare Simple Pizza Crust. Preheat oven to 350° F. While crust is rising, prepare Three Herb Pesto. Lightly brush a 14-inch pizza pan with olive oil. Shape dough to fit pizza pan. Spread pesto over dough and bake for 10 minutes.

Meanwhile, slice and core the tomatoes and shred the mozzarella. Remove pizza from oven and place on a heat-safe surface. Toss mozzarella and garlic together. Sprinkle the cheese and garlic mixture on the pizza. Distribute the tomatoes and olives evenly across the top of the the pizza. Return pizza to oven and bake for an additional 25 minutes or until crust is crisp. Serves 4 to 6.

Savory Pesto Frittata

A frittata is a simple and easy way to make a delicious, satisfying dish.

1 cup cubed new potatoes
1 cup cubed broccoli
1 cup cubed zucchini
1 cup cubed cauliflower
1/2 cup chopped Spanish or yellow onion
2 teaspoons each butter and olive oil
Summer Savory Pesto (page 38)
2 tablespoons warm water or cream
2 eggs
2/3 cup finely grated Monterey Jack cheese

Preheat oven to 325 °F. Cube the vegetables to a 1/2-inch size. Heat butter and oil in a sauté pan large enough for the Frittata. Sauté the vegetables briefly, stirring frequently, then add 4 tablespoons of water. Partially cover the pan and steam over a low heat until the vegetables are tender.

Thin 1/4 cup Summer Savory Pesto with 2 tablespoons of warm water or cream and sprinkle the mixture over the vegetables. Beat the eggs and pour over the vegetables. Sprinkle cheese over the top. Cover, and bake for 6 minutes or until cheese has melted and eggs have set. Serve hot in wedges, garnished with fresh parsley. Serves 4.

Fennel Vegetable Soufflé

A low-sided, pyrex baking dish makes a souffle cook quickly, creating a moist center, and a nicely browned crust. The fennel adds a unique twist to the vegetable and cheese flavors.

1 cup chopped broccoli stems and florets
1 cup chopped cauliflower stems and florets
1/2 cup Fennel Pesto (page 26)
1/2 cup ricotta cheese
1/4 cup freshly grated Parmesan cheese
4 eggs, separated
salt and freshly ground black pepper to taste
1 tablespoon freshly grated Parmesan cheese

Butter a 12-inch pyrex baking dish or four 1-1/4 cup individual soufflés and chill in the refrigerator. Cook the broccoli and cauliflower, covered, in boiling water or in the microwave until just tender. Drain well. Set aside about 1/2 cup broccoli and cauliflower florets.

Place the broccoli, cauliflower, pesto, ricotta, 1/4 cup Parmesan cheese, and egg yolks in a food processor or blender. Blend on high until a smooth texture is achieved. Season to taste with salt and freshly ground black pepper. Add the reserved broccoli and cauliflower florets and pulse a few times, leaving some pieces for texture.

Preheat the oven to 450°F. In a separate bowl,

whip the egg whites with an electric mixer just until they form soft peaks. Stir a third of the egg whites into the broccoli mixture. Fold in the remainder, deflating the whites as little as possible. Fill the pyrex dish or small soufflé cups to the rim. Sprinkle with the remaining 1 tablespoon of Parmesan cheese. Place on a baking sheet. Bake the large soufflé approximately 15 to 18 minutes and the individual soufflés 10 to 12 minutes, until nicely browned and still moist in the center. Small souffles can be unmolded, if desired, and served with a cheese sauce. Serve hot. Serves 4.

Baked Sole with Watercress Pesto Sauce

2 tablespoons butter
1 tablespoon olive oil
1/3 cup minced green pepper
1 large shallot, minced
1-1/2 cups chopped mushrooms
salt and freshly ground pepper to taste
1 fresh tomato, thinly sliced
1 pound sole fillets
1/2 cup Basil Watercress Pesto (page 20)
3 tablespoons light cream

Preheat oven to 350°F. In a sauté pan, heat the butter and oil and sauté the pepper and shallots for 2 minutes. Add the chopped mushrooms and continue to sauté until the mushrooms begin to soften. Season to taste with salt and pepper. Layer half the sole fillets in a lightly oiled, low-sided baking dish. Cover with the pepper, shallots, and mushrooms. Place slices of tomato over all. Layer the remaining sole fillets on top and cover with foil. Bake for 15 minutes. Meanwhile, combine the pesto with enough cream to make a thick pourable sauce. Cover the sole with the pesto sauce, return to the oven, and bake uncovered until the sauce is bubbly, about 5 minutes. Serve hot. Serves 4.

Basil Rice Casserole

The onions are the basis for the French-style sauce which enlivens this easy-to-make rice dish.

2 quarts salted water
1/2 cup long-grain white rice
2 tablespoons butter
1/2 cup Classic Basil Pesto (page 17)
4 cups roughly chopped yellow onions
salt and freshly ground black pepper to taste
1/4 cup grated Swiss cheese
1/4 cup light cream

Preheat the oven to 325 °F. Bring the water to a brisk boil. Add the rice and boil uncovered for about 5 minutes. Drain and set aside. Melt the butter with the pesto in a large pan. Stir in the chopped onions, rice, and freshly ground pepper and salt. Mix well, until everything is coated with the butter-pesto mixture.

Place in a shallow pyrex baking dish. Cover tightly with heavy foil and bake for 40 to 50 minutes, stirring once or twice, until the rice is tender. Remove and stir in grated cheese and cream. Season with salt and freshly ground black pepper to taste. Serve immediately. Serves 4 to 6.

Grilled Lemon Chicken with Bowties

This is a light pasta dish that will get rave reviews. Made with grilled chicken, it has that sublime flavor that comes only from cooking over flame. This recipe works best if you have one person to grill the chicken and one person to make the sauce and pasta. The sauce should be ready for the chicken as soon as it comes off the grill.

3 tablespoons lime juice
3 tablespoons Roses lime juice
1/4 cup Lemon Basil Pesto (page 24)
3 tablespoons virgin olive oil
1/4 teaspoon coarsely ground pepper
2 skinless, double chicken breasts
1 pound dry or fresh bowtie pasta
1/4 cup butter
3/4 cup sour cream
3/4 cup milk
2/3 cup freshly grated Parmesan cheese
3/4 cup sliced mushrooms
1/2 cup chopped scallions (tops included)
2 cups broccoli florets
salt and freshly ground black pepper to taste

Coat grill with non-stick vegetable spray. Preheat gas grill or start briquettes, leaving the lid on. The

grill needs to be <u>HOT</u> to properly seal the juice into the meat.

Combine lime juice, Roses lime juice, Lemon Basil Pesto, pepper, and olive oil in a small microwave dish, and cook on high for about 1 minute, or long enough for it to boil briefly. Trim all fat from the chicken breasts. Using a basting brush, paint the breasts with the pesto mixture being sure to deposit bits of pepper on the chicken. Place chicken breasts on grill and cover again, cooking for about 3 minutes, or long enough to sear lines into the breasts. Paint the tops of the breasts, turn, then paint the seared side. Turn again after about 5 minutes, changing the angle to sear a nice cross pattern into the breasts, painting before and after each turn. After both sides have been turned twice, remove from grill and shred into bite-sized chunks with two forks.

Meanwhile, cook bowties in until al dente, and drain. In a large sauté pan, melt butter and add sour cream and milk. Simmer gently, stirring constantly for 3 minutes. Slowly add cheese, stirring constantly. Place mushrooms, scallions, and broccoli in a ceramic dish and dot with a pat of butter. Cook, covered with plastic wrap, in the microwave on high for 4 minutes. Immediately add vegetables to sauce along with shredded chicken breast. Stir to coat with sauce and season to taste with salt and freshly ground black pepper.

Place pasta on individual plates and top with sauce. Pass with freshly grated Parmesan cheese. Serves 4 to 6.

Oysters with Lemon Sorrel Sauce

For the best flavor, buy and cook oysters the day they arrive at your fish market.

4 pounds very fresh, large Pacific oysters
1/2 cup Basil Sorrel Pesto (page 21)
1 teaspoon lemon juice
1 teaspoon Roses Lime juice
3/4 cup dry breadcrumbs

Combine Basil Sorrel Pesto, lemon juice, Roses Lime juice and breadcrumbs in a small bowl. Whisk together thoroughly.

Scrub the oysters well under cool running water. Discard any opened oysters. Bring about 2 inches of water to a boil in a large covered pan. Add the oysters and simmer for 15 minutes until they just crack open. Drain in a colander.

Crack the shells apart by inserting a paring knife between the two halves and discard the top shell. Arrange the opened shells on baking dish. Place under a hot broiler for about 4 minutes until the edges curl. Remove from broiler and spoon 1/2 to 3/4 teaspoon of the pesto sauce over each oyster. If the sauce is too thick to spread, thin with a little olive oil. Serve hot. Serves 4 to 6.

Pesto Snapper Kabobs

This colorful grilled fish kobob goes well over wild rice garnished with fresh lemon slices and tarragon sprigs and served with chilled Chardonay.

1 tablespoon lemon juice
2 tablespoons butter
2 tablespoons chopped whole scallions
2 tablespoons French Tarragon Pesto (page 43)
salt and freshly ground black pepper to taste
2 pounds Red Snapper fillets, cut in 1-1/2 inch pieces
1 sweet red pepper, seeded and sliced
1 green pepper, seeded and sliced

Prepare briquettes or preheat gas grill. Prepare marinade by placing lemon juice, butter, scallions, salt and pepper in a small bowl; microwave on high for 1 minute. Then whisk in French Tarragon Pesto.

Skewer snapper pieces alternately with slices of red and green peppers. Coat the grill with non-stick vegetable spray. Using a basting brush, paint the kabobs with the marinade, and place on the grill. Grill for 6 to 8 minutes, brushing with the marinade, and turning occasionally. Test a piece of fish; it should be moist and tender. Serve hot with any remaining marinade poured over the kabobs. Serves 4 to 6.

Grilled Salmon with Lemon Basil Sauce

This lemony marinade gives this barbequed salmon its tart, smokey flavor.

> **1/4 cup Lemon Basil Pesto (page 24)**
> **3 tablespoons lemon juice**
> **3 tablespoons Roses Lime juice**
> **1/4 cup olive oil**
> **1/4 teaspoon Beau monde seasoning**
> **salt and freshly ground pepper to taste**
> **2 (3/4 pound) fresh salmon fillets (skin on)**
> **1 large tomato, cut in 1/2-inch slices**

Whisk together the pesto, lemon and lime juices, olive oil, salt, Beau monde and freshly ground pepper to make marinade. Wash the salmon thoroughly in hot water to remove the fishy odor. In a shallow ceramic dish, marinate overnight in the refrigerator, turning the fish at least once.

Coat the grill with non-stick vegetable spray and preheat. Place salmon, skin side down on a medium-hot grill. Grill for 10 to 12 minutes with lid down. Carefully move to serving platter using two spatulas. Place tomato slices on the grill, turning once so grill marks appear on both sides. Bring remaining marinade just to a boil in a saucepan. Arrange tomatoes around salmon and top with marinade. Serves 4.

Emerald Scallops with Arugula Crumbs

*This pesto retains more of a green color than tradition-
al basil pestos. Serve this dish with a light saffron rice
topped with grilled red peppers for a colorful main
course.*

> **1-1/3 pounds fresh bay scallops**
> **1 small lemon**
> **1/4 cup sweet butter, at room temperature**
> **l/4 cup Emerald Arugula Pesto (page 28)**
> **2/3 cup dry bread crumbs**
> **salt**
> **lemon wedges**

Preheat the oven to 450°F. Wash scallops thoroughly in hot water to remove fishy odor, and place
in a single layer in a lightly oiled baking dish.
Squeeze lemon juice over all.

Blend together the butter and pesto in a small
bowl. Add bread crumbs until the mixture has a
crumbly texture. Season to taste with salt. Spoon
the topping over the scallops. Bake for about 7
minutes until just barely hot and bubbly. Turn up
heat to broil and cook for another 3 minutes so the
top is just a little brown and crunchy. Serve hot
with lemon wedges on the side. Serves 6.

Pesto Vegetable Bake

The bacon adds extra flavor and texture to this vegetable main course. Serve with crusty garlic bread.

2 cups cubed yellow squash (1/2-inch)
2 cups sliced green beans (1/2-inch)
2 cups cubed zucchini (1/2-inch)
3 tablespoons minced red onion
1/2 cup red bell pepper, chopped
6 to 8 slices bacon
3 tablespoons butter
3 tablespoons Three Herb Pesto (page 31)
salt and freshly ground pepper to taste
1/2 cup grated Monterey jack cheese

Preheat the oven to 350°F. Chop bacon, cook until crispy, drain, and set aside. Steam the squash, green beans, and zucchini until barely tender, 5 to 6 minutes. Combine with the onion and red pepper in a large bowl. Melt the butter and add to the pesto; mix in bacon. Pour over the vegetables. Add salt and pepper to taste and toss lightly. Transfer to a low-sided baking dish. Cover with foil and bake for 20 minutes. Remove from the oven and top with grated cheese. Return to oven and bake, uncovered until lightly brown, about 5 minutes. Serve hot. Serves 4.

Chapter 5

More About Basil and Other Pesto Ingredients

About Basil

Basil, the basis of many pestos, comes in innumerable varieties, each with a unique aroma and taste, adding subtle nuances to pesto. Fortunately, if you are a gardener, you'll find that basil grows as well basking in American sunshine as it does in the Mediterranean where hillsides are covered with a wild, small-leaf basil that people pick at will.

The most common basil, **sweet basil** *(Ocimum basilicum)*, has bright green, shiny, slightly serrated leaves and whorls of white blossoms. The plant usually attains about 3 feet in height with leaves that are 2-1/2 inches long. Its flavor is robust and spicy with minty undertones.

A larger leafed Japanese variety called **lettuce leaf basil** has curly, puckered leaves resembling those of curly leafed lettuce. Its flavor is more mild than sweet basil, although it may be used interchangeably. Add the leaves to salads or use as wrappers for savory fillings such as grilled or boiled shrimp, spicy shredded chicken or pork, chopped vegetables or tabbouleh.

Smaller leafed basils also are culinary staples. French cooks especially favor **French fine leaf basil**, whose numerous 1/4-inch leaves have an enticing sweetness. This 1-1/2-foot tall, bushy plant grows well in pots.

A similar plant, **bush basil**, reaches about 12 inches in height with small, slightly rounded, clove-

scented leaves; tiny bouquets of these leaves make dainty garnishes.

Spicy **globe basil** grows about 1 foot tall in a uniquely round shape, and its prolific white blossoms make it a valuable ornamental plant.

Italian cooks prefer **picolo verde fino**, a basil with narrow dark green leaves, and many agree that its sweet and spicy flavor is best for making pesto. This is a tall plant (2-1/2 feet) that likes some elbow room.

Lemon basil, has pale green, pointed leaves (approximately 1-inch long and 1-inch wide) that are slightly hairy with a prominent and delicious lemon scent. In fact, its lemony aroma actually masks that of basil. A pesto flavored with lemon basil and ground almonds is quite extraordinary tasting. This variety of basil seems to seed very quickly so keep seed heads pinched continually.

The deep purple color of dark **opal basil** gives good contrast in the garden as well as in food. Most notable, however, is the rich ruby color it gives to vinegar. A delicious and colorful pesto made with dark opal basil and sun-dried tomatoes may be used with pasta or in a cheese torta. Dark opal basil usually reaches about 1 foot in height with leaves that are 2-1/2 inches long and 1-1/2 inches wide. It has serrated leaves and lovely lavender flowers tinged with deeper purple.

"Purple Ruffles" basil retains its deep and true purple color without fading. Its crinkly and serrated leaves provide color and texture in the garden and make unusual garnishes and bouquets. 'Purple

Ruffles' may be used similarly to dark opal basil in cooking.

Despite the many varieties of basils, they all require basically the same growing conditions. Plenty of warm sunshine is imperative for these sun worshippers. Although they like a slightly moist and rich soil, it is essential that it drains well. Basil is an herb that is easily grown from seed since it germinates in a few days; however, do not attempt to plant seeds during a cold, damp spring. Wait until warm soil and air temperatures allow the seeds to germinate properly; cool temperatures stunt the plants.

Harvesting Fresh Herbs

Basil and other fresh herbs bruise and darken easily when harvested, so only pick just the amount you need. Overzealous gardeners too often cram the kitchen sink full of freshly picked herbs, bruising tender leaves or allowing them to stand too long in water. To their dismay, many of the leaves blacken.

When harvesting most herbs, spray the leaves gently with the hose in the early morning to remove any debris, then allow them to dry naturally in the sunshine. After harvesting, take them to the kitchen, discard any damaged leaves, and proceed with your favorite recipe.

Other Pesto Herbs

Arugula

The wavy, green leaves of arugula resemble oak-leaf lettuce or radish and have a peppery, nutty taste. It's white flowers are streaked with crimson when the plant is about 2 feet tall. Arugula plants have dotted the rocky hillsides of the Mediterranean for centuries and have long been used as a salad green. In fact, in Italy and Sicily, arugula grows wild and makes a favorite "poor man's salad." Pesto made with arugula retains its bright green color. This herb is as easy to grow from seed as radishes and grows well with plenty of sunshine.

Cilantro

This fresh herb grown from coriander seeds resembles Italian flat-leafed parsley in appearance but it has a unique aroma and pungency that often demands an acquired taste. It is frequently used in Southwestern-style cooking to flavor salsas, beans and other south-of-the-border dishes. Cooks from China, Thailand, the Middle East and the Mediterranean have found ways to use this herb to compliment their unique styles. Plant seeds from September through February to be assured of healthy plants by early spring.

Fennel

Fennel, a native of the Mediterranean, resembles dill with bright green, feathery foliage. However, the subtle anise flavor and scent are unmistakably different. Its foliage, bulbous base, and seeds have been used in cooking and baking from Italy to India to Sweden. Plant seeds in the fall towards the back of the garden, because common fennel grows quite tall with a lovely plumage.

Garlic Chives

Garlic chives, also known as Oriental garlic or Chinese chives *(gow choy)* grow taller than common onion chives with flat, light green, reed-like leaves boasting delicate clusters of star-like white flowers that are especially pretty as a garnish. Their tender, new leaves have a tasty, mild garlic flavor that is valued for stir-frys, sautéed vegetables, and as a garnish. Plant chives from nursery seedlings in pots or in the ground. They are a perennial, so don't disturb them when they are dormant.

Oregano

This hardy perennial has oval to elliptical leaves that are slightly hairy underneath with a robust and aromatic scent. The flowers range from white to mauvish-purple. This herb is used throughout the Mediterranean and is especially favored by Italians for hearty tomato sauces and pasta dishes. In the Middle East it is used to flavor eggplant and other vegetables. Mexicans add it to their spicy

chile sauces and stews. Of course, in America it is the popular pizza herb. Plant several varieties from nursery seedlings, making sure to pinch off a few leaves and rubbing them gently to test for aroma and flavor before purchase.

Rosemary

This native Mediterranean herb comes in both upright and creeping varieties. It has leathery, highly aromatic needle-like leaves and lovely blue flowers that sprout along woody stems. In Spain and Italy, it has been used for centuries to flavor lamb, goat, veal, chicken, and game. Seeds are difficult to germinate, so purchase seedling plants from a nursery.

Sage

Sage leaves come in a variety of colors from grayish-green to purple. The pebbly, elongated leaves are highly aromatic and sprout from shrub-like woody stems. This perennial has double-lipped violet flowers that bloom in early spring. In America sage is known mostly as a dried herb that is taken down from the spice rack to season the turkey stuffing once a year. This highly aromatic fresh herb has been a favorite of Mediterranean cooks for pasta and potato dishes. French and English chefs use it for wild game and fowl and for flavoring cheese and breads. Seeds are difficult to germinate, so purchase seedling plants from a nursery.

Tarragon

Tarragon is a small perennial wormwood grown for its pungent aromatic foliage used traditionally as a flavoring for making pickles and vinegar. French Tarragon, the variety most highly prized by cooks, has a tangy, anise-flavored overtone. The demand for French tarragon exceeds the supply because tarragon has become more popular in modern cooking and is difficult to propagate. The plant is only propagated by divisions of the root of second-year plants or from cuttings taken in mid-summer. Cuttings take two months to root and must be carried through the winter for spring planting.

Thyme

The slightly pointed, highly aromatic leaves of thyme range from glossy dark green to wooly silver or variegated green and gold. Tiny star-like flowers bloom throughout the summer in shades from crimson to pink to white. In Europe, thyme is the legendary romantic herb of fairies and young maidens, and is used in peasant fare to *haute cuisine*. Creole, Cajun, and Mexican cooks also favor this herb. The dry rocky hillsides of the Mediterranean are this herb's homeland and chef's of this region use thyme to flavor poultry, lamb, and beef as well as sautéd vegetables and cheese. Grow this plant from seeds, cuttings, or root divisions and tend it carefully during hot, humid summers.

Suppliers of Herbs and Specialty Food Products

Angelica Herb and Spice
137 Ist Avenue
New York, NY 10003
212-677-1549
herbs

Balducci's
Mail Order Division
334 East 11th Street
New York, NY 10003
(800) 822-1444
specialty foods

Companion Plants
7247 N. Coolville Ridge Road
Athens, OH 45701
(614) 592-4643
herb plants and seeds

Corti Brothers
Carmichael, CA 95608
(916) 483-6452
pasta and other Italian foods

Dean & Deluca
110 Green Street, Suite 304
New York, NY 10012
(212) 431-1691
(800) 221-7714
specialty foods

DeLaurenti
1435 First Ave.
Seattle, WA 98101
(206) 622-0141
specialty foods

Figi's, Inc.
3200 South Maple Ave.
Marshfield, WI 54449
(715) 384-6101
smoked meats, cheeses

Fox Hill Farm
444 West Michigan Avenue
P.O. Box 9
Parma, MI 49269
(517) 531-3179
300 herb varieties, basil festival

Gaston Dupre, Inc.
7904 Hopi Place
Tampa, FL 33634
(813) 885-9445
all types of pasta

Glie Farms
1600 Bathgate Avenue
Bronx, NY 10457
(212) 731-2130
herbs

Golden Meadows Herb Farm
431 South Street Augustine
Dallas, TX 75217
(214) 398-3479
herb plants, dried herbs

The Herb Shop
278 South Main
Springville, UT 84663
(801) 489-8787
herbs

House of Quality Herbs
P.O. Box 14
Woodland Hills, CA 91365
herbs

Harrington's Ham Company
Main Street
Richmonds, VT 05477
(802) 434-4444
meats, cheeses, and gourmet items

Hemlock Hill Herb Farm
Hemlock Hill Road
Litchfield, CT 06759
(203) 567-5031
herb plants

House of Spices
7617 Broadway
Jackson Heights, NY 11373
(718) 476-1577
spices

It's About Thyme
P.O. Box 878-HH
Manchacha, TX 78652
(512) 280-1192
herb plants

Lambs Farm
P.O. Box 520
Libertyville, IL 60048
(708) 362-4636
cheeses, breads, gourmet items

Logee's Greenhouses
55 North Street
Danielson, CT 06239
herb plants

Manganaro Foods
488 Ninth Avenue
New York, NY 10018
(212) 563-7748
Italian specialties

Nature's Herb Company
281 Ellis Street
San Francisco, CA 94102
(415) 474-2756
herbs

Nichols Herb & Rare Seeds
1190 North Pacific Highway
Albany, OR 97321
(503) 928-9280
*herb plants, seeds, unusual
varieties cilantro and basil*

Paradise Farms
P.O. Box 436
Summerland, CA 93067
Write for recipe booklet($7.00)
*organically grown herbs and edible
flowers*

Redwood City Seed Company
P.O. Box 361
Redwood City, CA 94064
(415) 325-7333
herb seeds, rare and unusual seeds

G. B. Ratto International Grocers
821 Washington Street
Oakland, CA 94607
*gourmet items, oils, vinegars,
spices, garlic strands, send for
catalog*

The Sandy Mush Herb Nursery
Route 2, Surrett Cove Road
Leicester, NC 28748
*over 600 unusual and common
herbs, seeds*

Select Origins, Inc.
Box N
Southhampton, NY 11968
(800) 822-2092
*herb & spice blends, vinegars, oils,
gourmet items*

Sheperd's Garden Seeds
6116 Highway 9, Dept. HH
Felton, CA 95018
(408) 335-5400
*herbs, many varieties of basil,
edible flowers*

Simon David
7117 Inwood Road
Austin, TX 75209
(214) 352-1781
*fresh herbs, edible flowers,
exotic condiments*

Sunnybrook Farms
9448 Mayfield Road
P.O. Box 6
Chesterland, OH 44026
(216) 729-7232
herb plants and seeds

Taylor's Herb Gardens, Inc.
1535 Lone Oak Road
Vista, CA 92084
(619) 727-3485
fresh herbs

Todaro Brothers
Mail-order Department
555 Second Avenue
New York, NY 10016
(212) 532-0633
Italian specialty foods

Well Sweep Herb Farm
317 Mount Bethel Road
Port Murray, NJ 07865
herb plants, write for catalog